FUCK LOVE HALLOWEEN

COLORING BOOK

SWEAR WORD EDITION

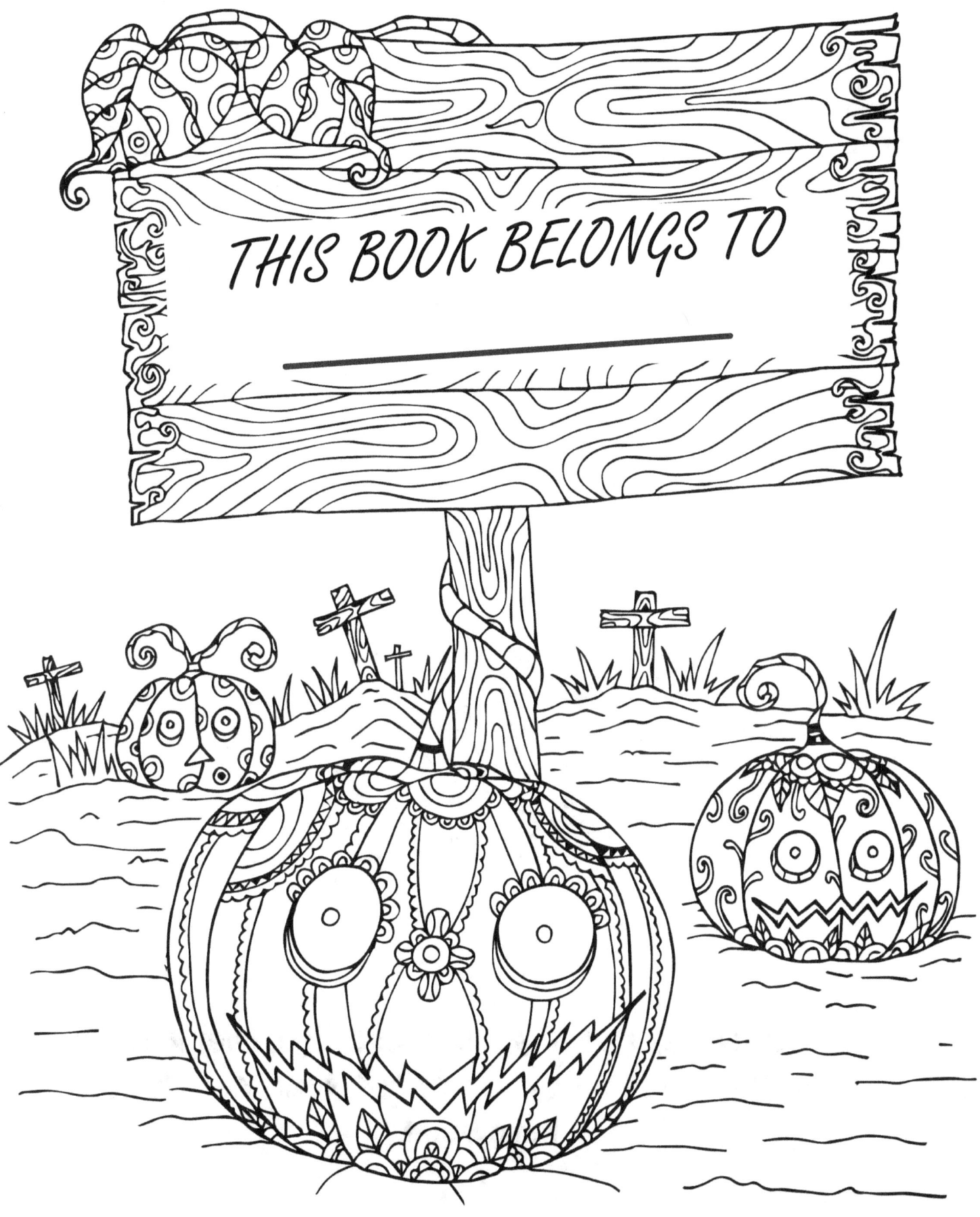

THIS BOOK BELONGS TO

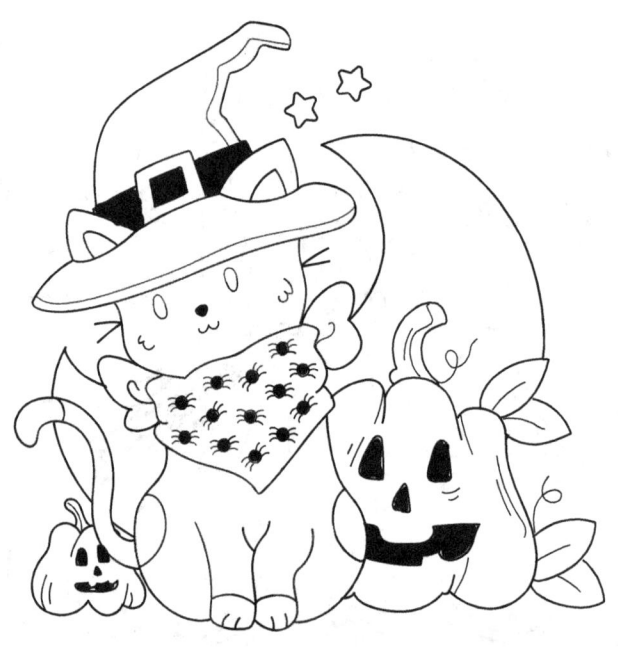

"If human Beings haD genuine Courage, they'D wear their Costumes every Day of the year, not just on Halloween."

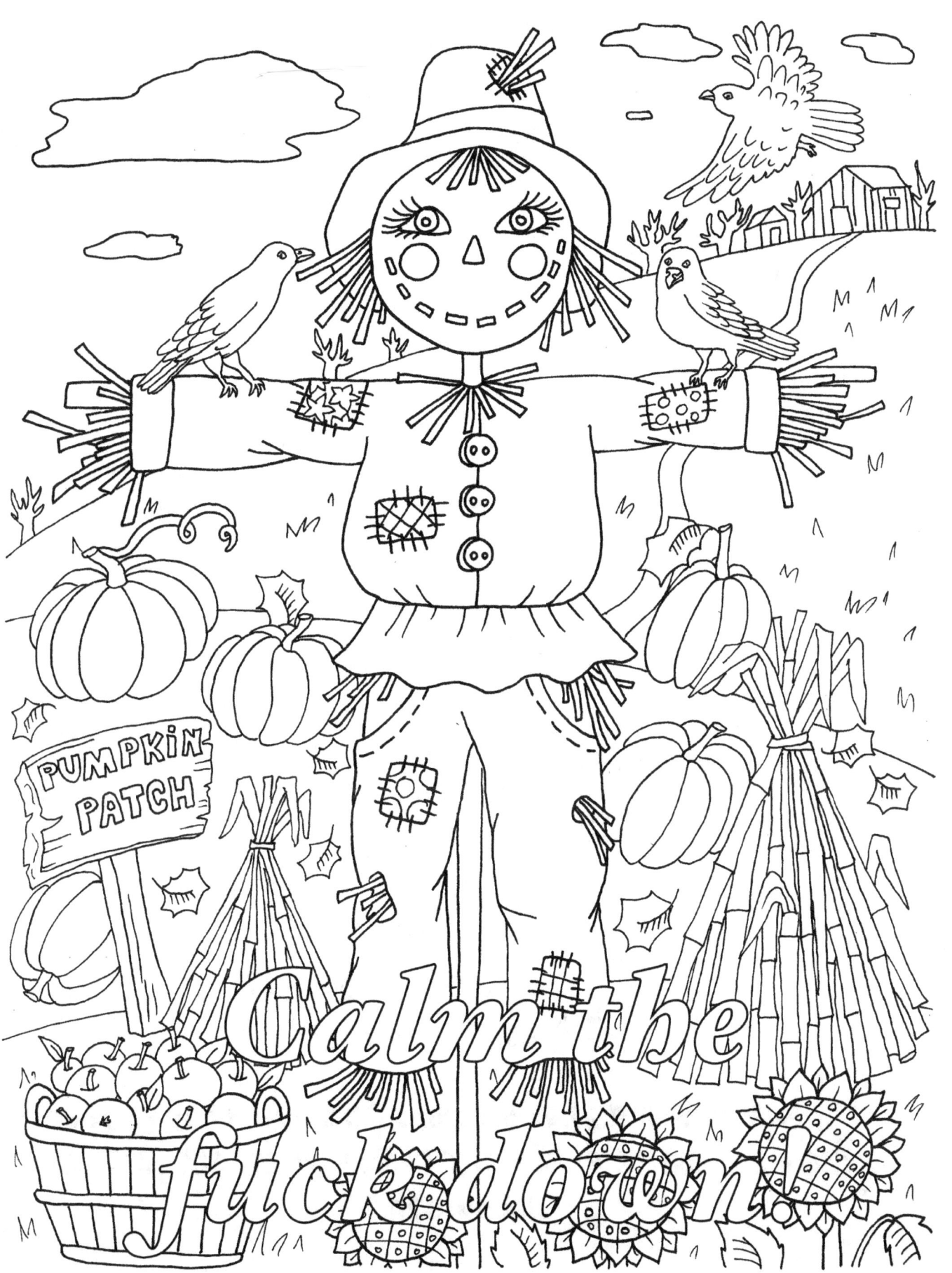

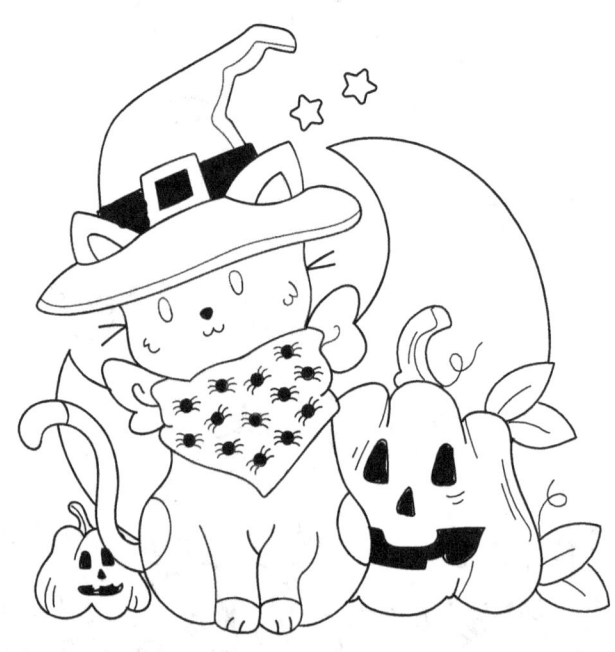

"If human Beings had genuine Courage, they'D wear their Costumes every Day of the year, not just on Halloween."

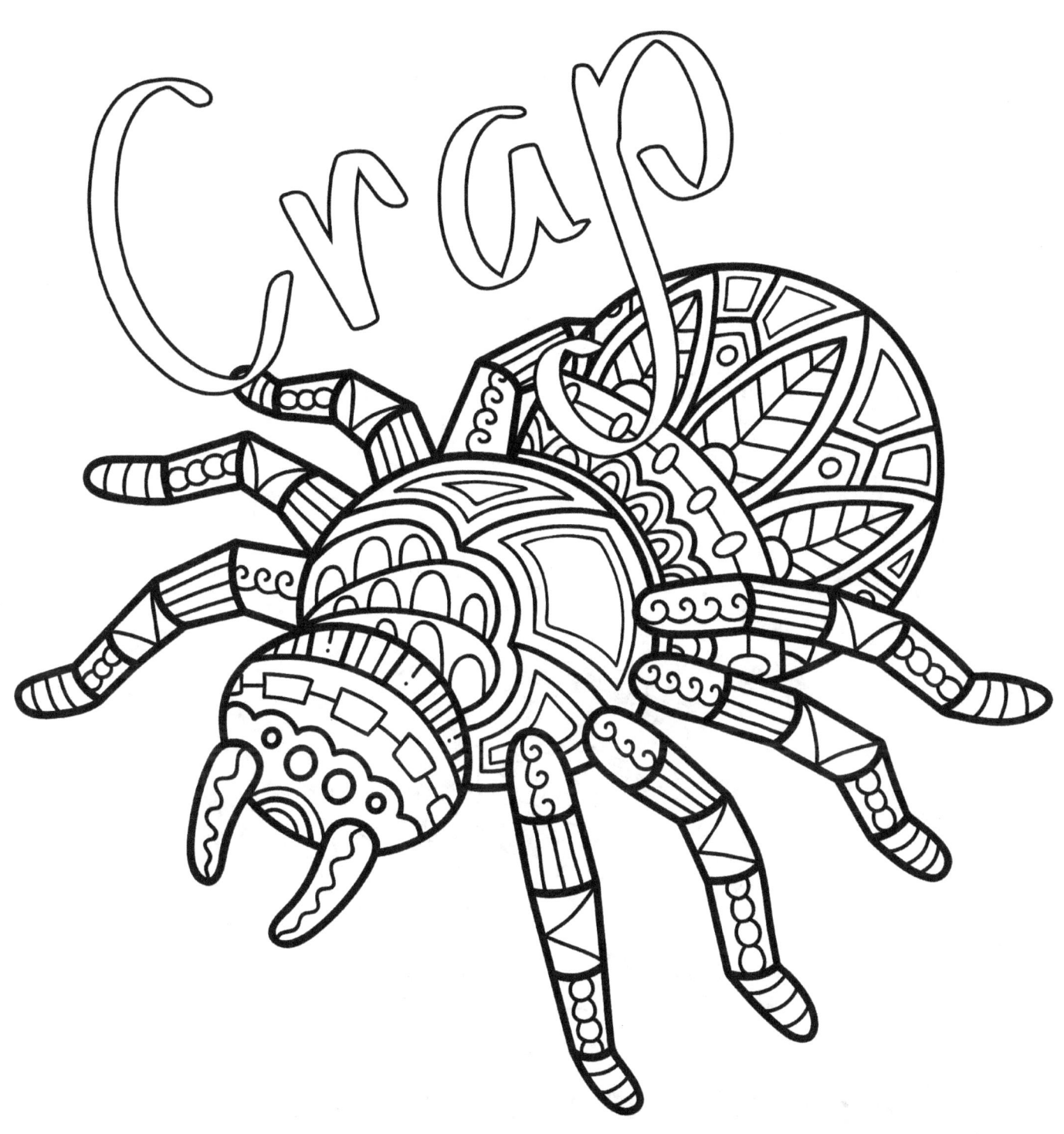

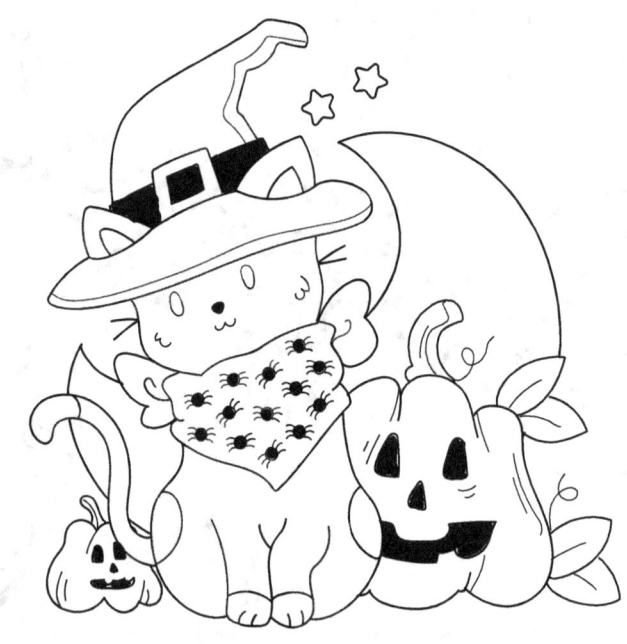

"If human Beings had genuine Courage, they'D wear their Costumes every Day of the year, not just on Halloween."

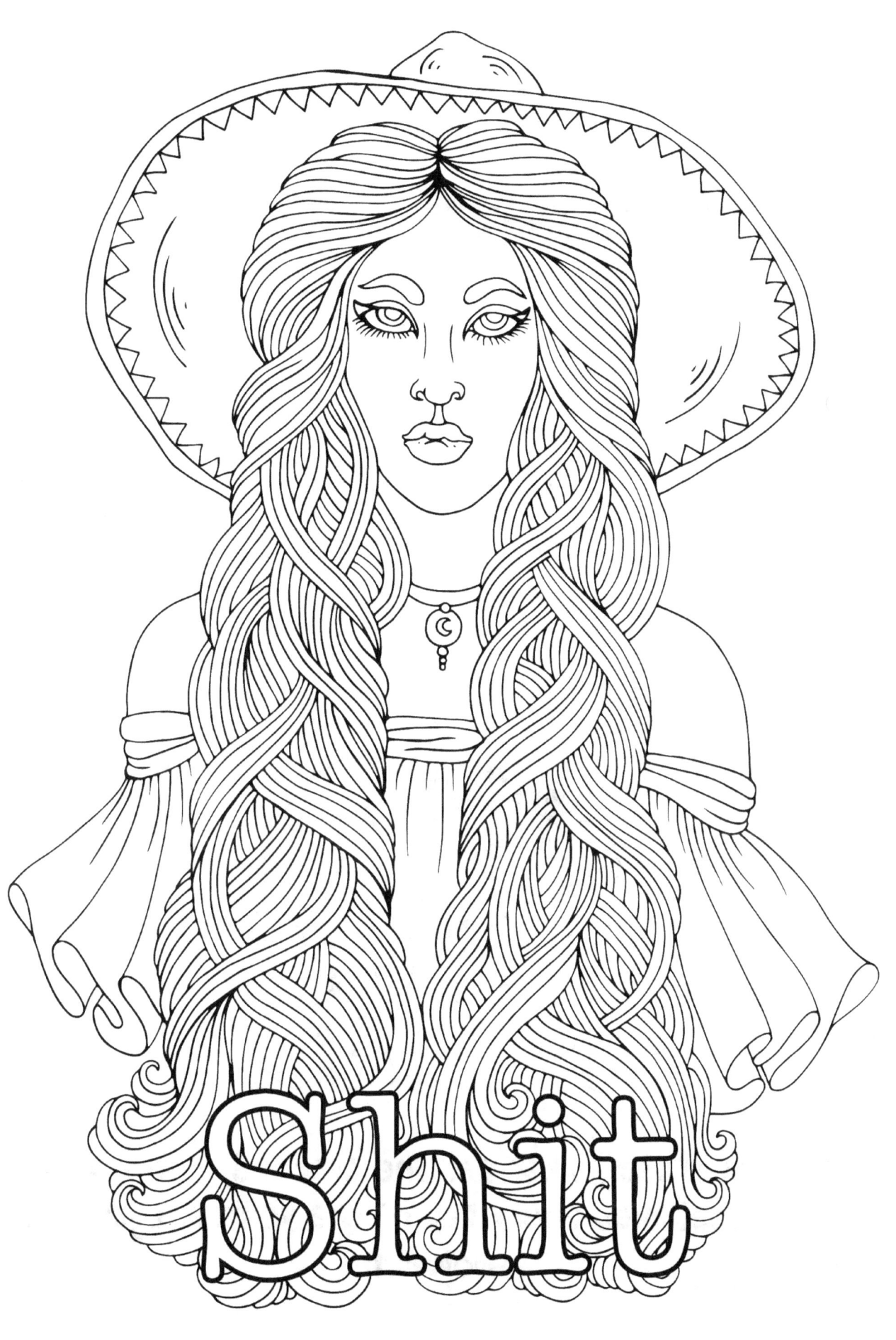

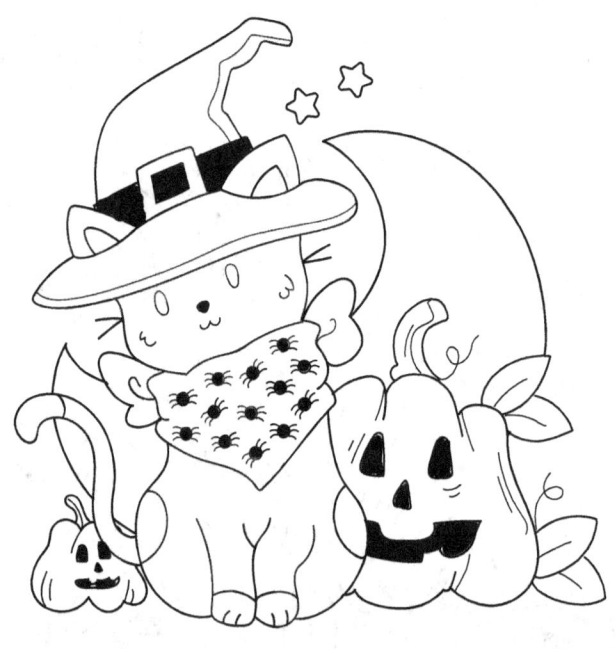

"If human Beings haD genuine Courage, they'D wear their Costumes every Day of the year, not just on Halloween."

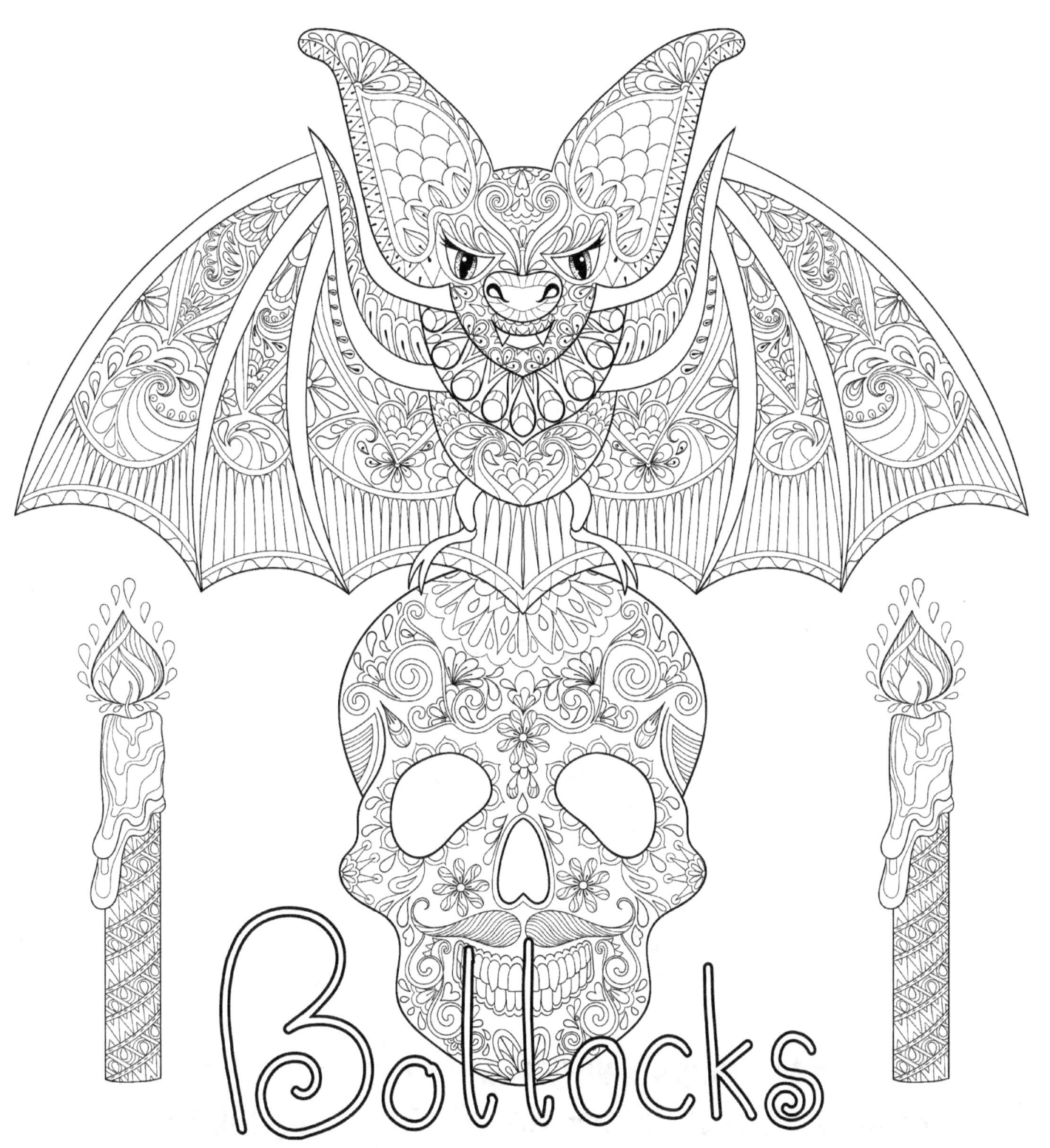

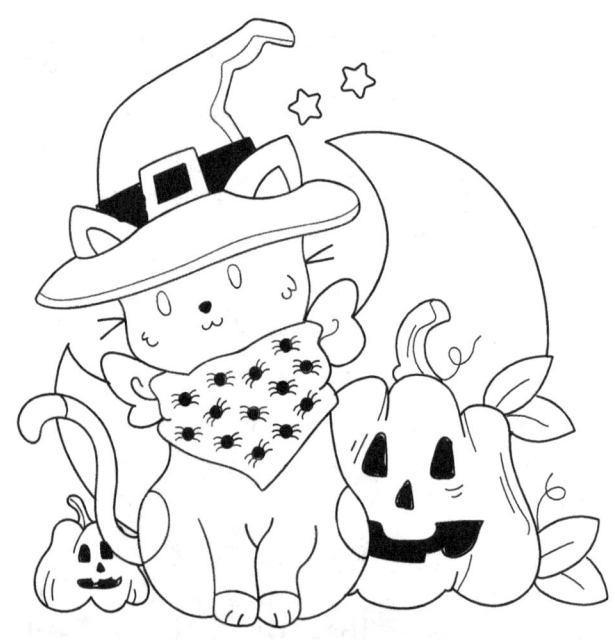

"If human Beings had genuine Courage, they'D wear their Costumes every Day of the year, not just on Halloween."

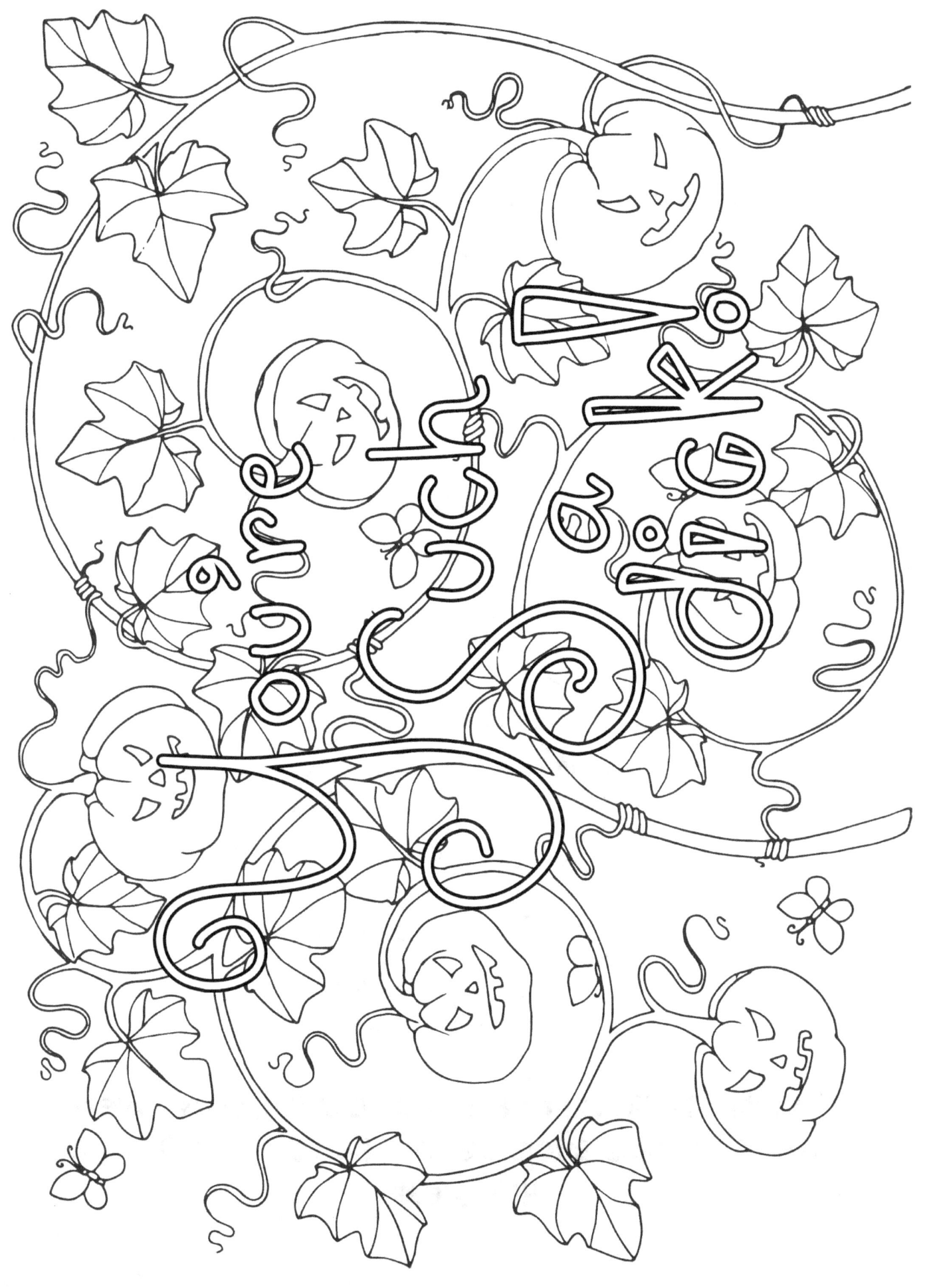

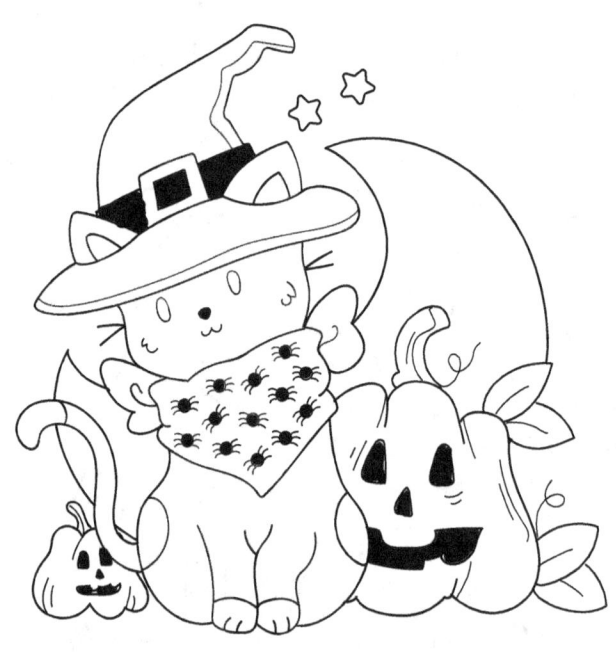

"If human Beings had genuine Courage, they'd wear their Costumes every Day of the year, not just on Halloween."

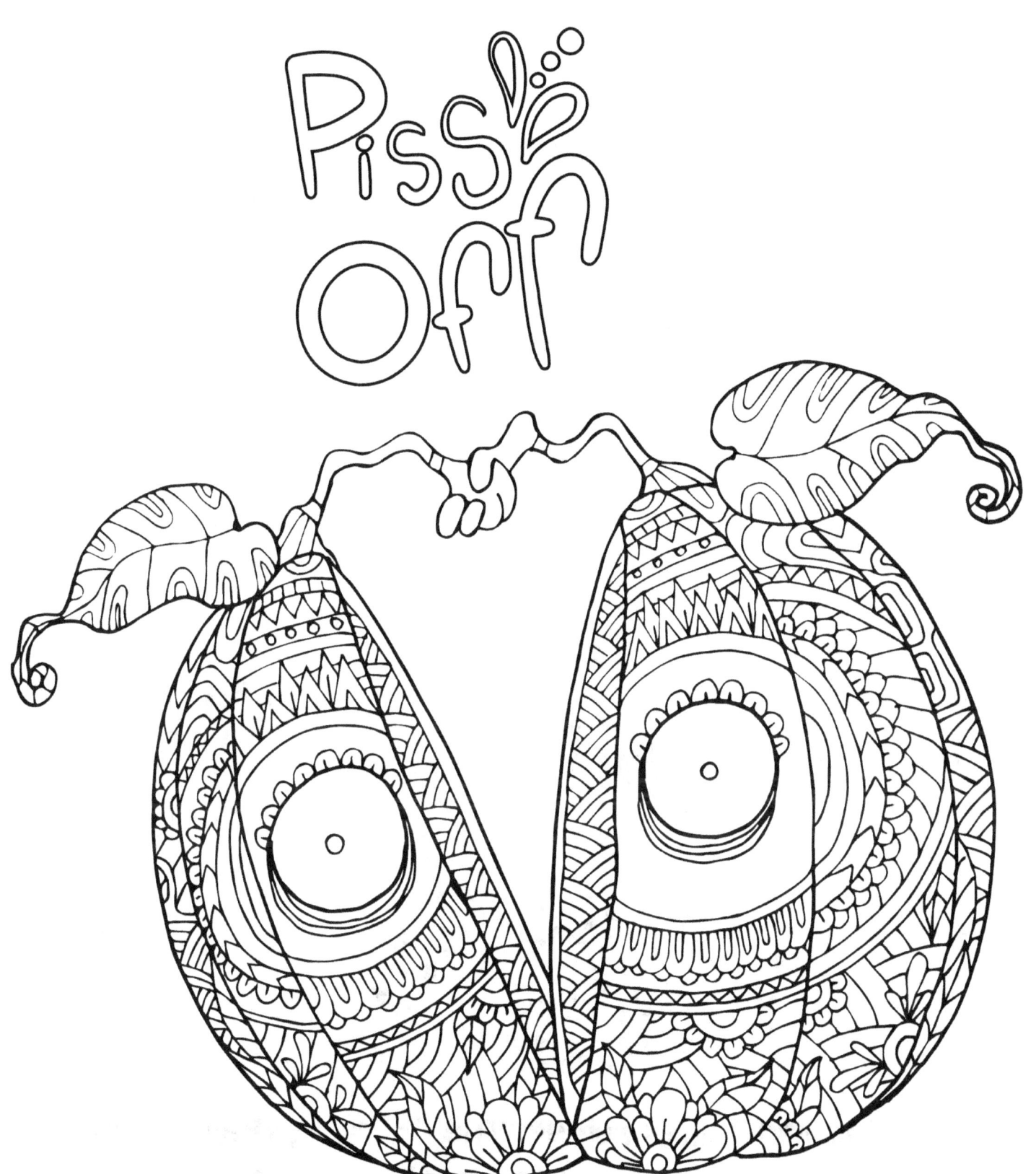

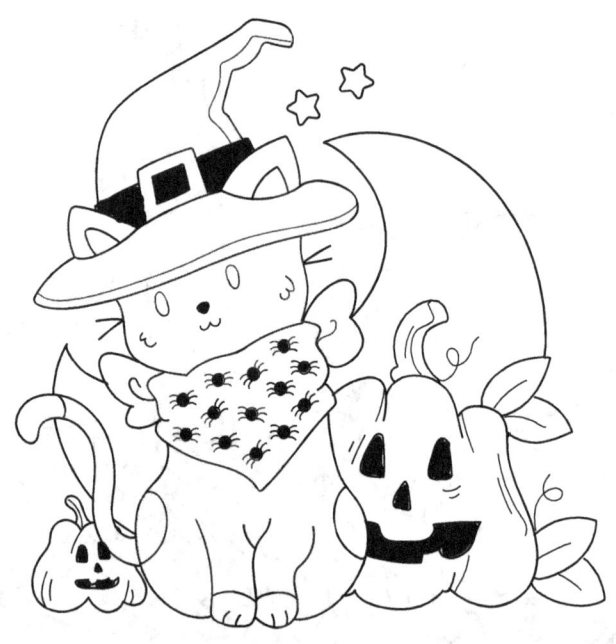

"If human Beings had genuine Courage, they'D wear their Costumes every Day of the year, not just on Halloween."

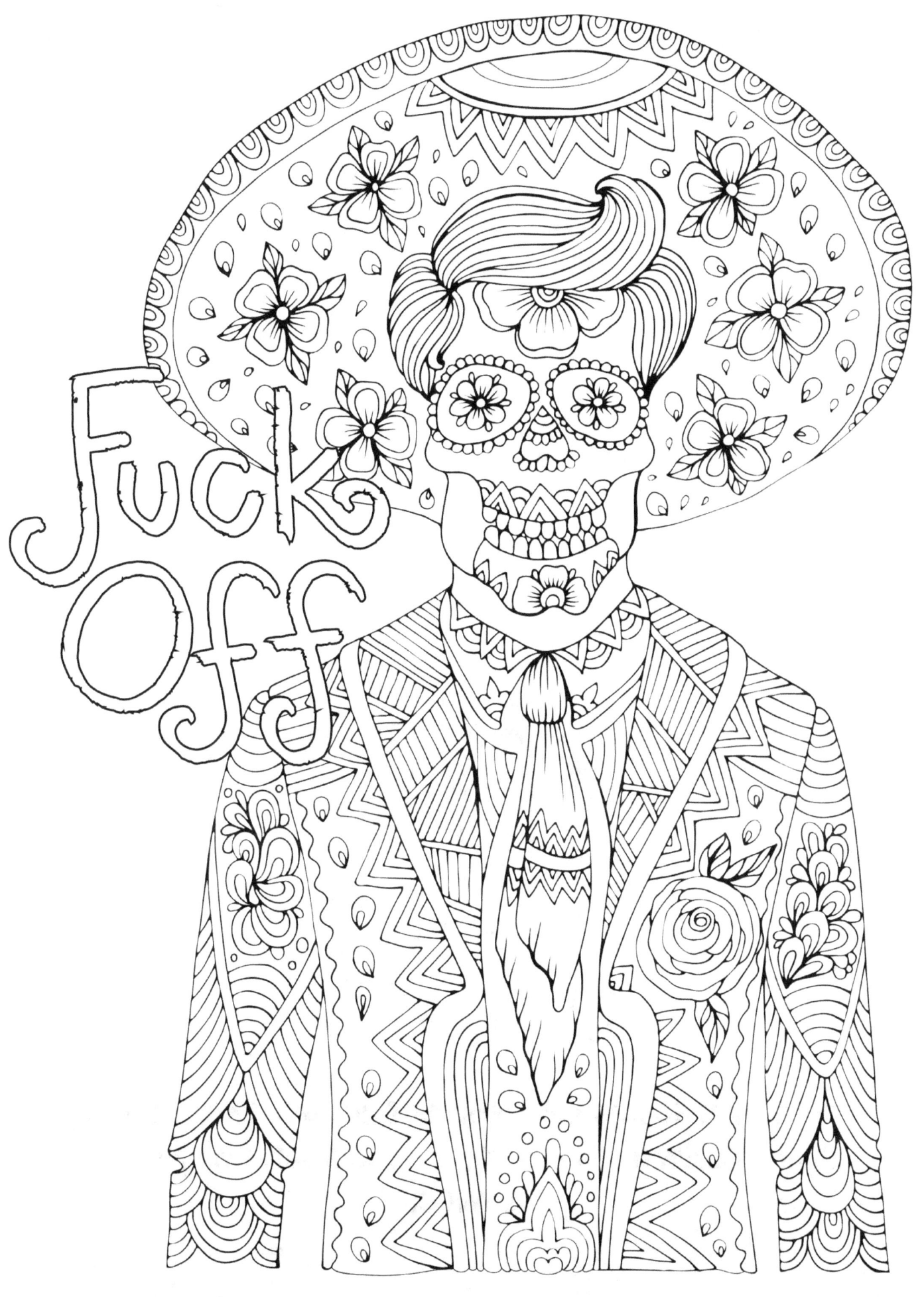

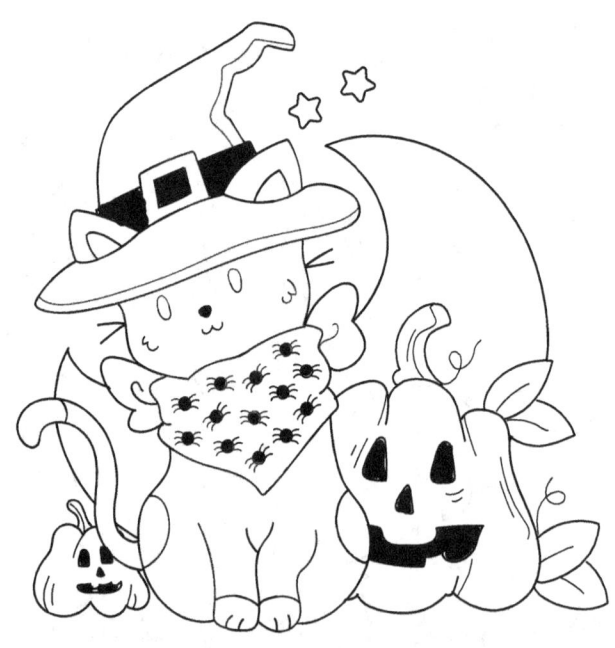

"If human Beings haD genuine Courage, they'D wear their Costumes every Day of the year, not just on Halloween."

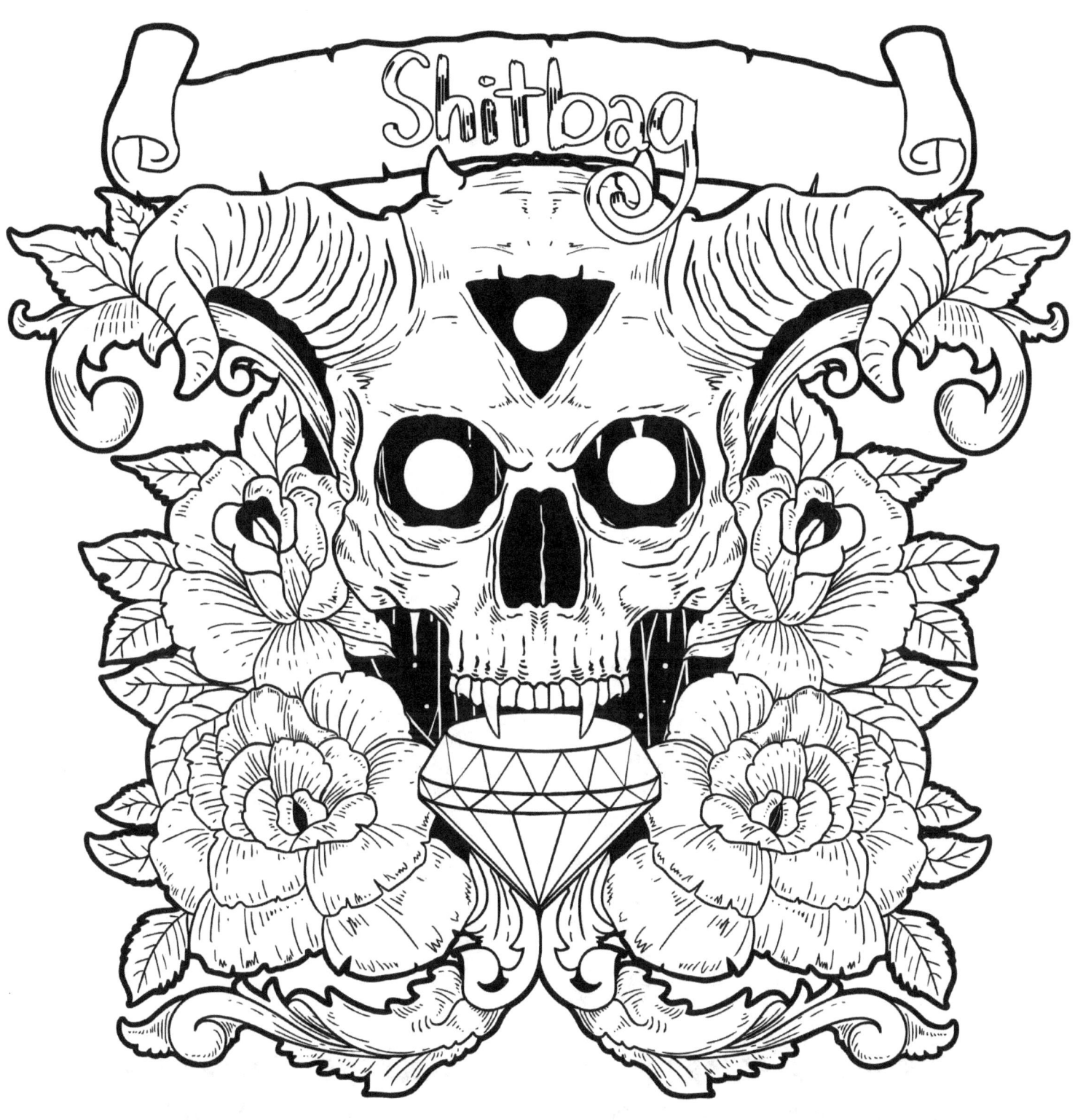

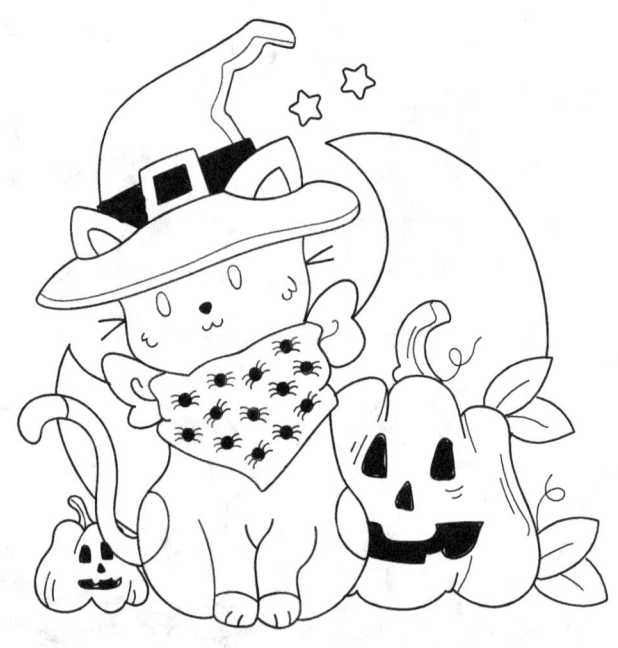

"If human Beings had genuine Courage, they'D wear their Costumes every Day of the year, not just on Halloween."

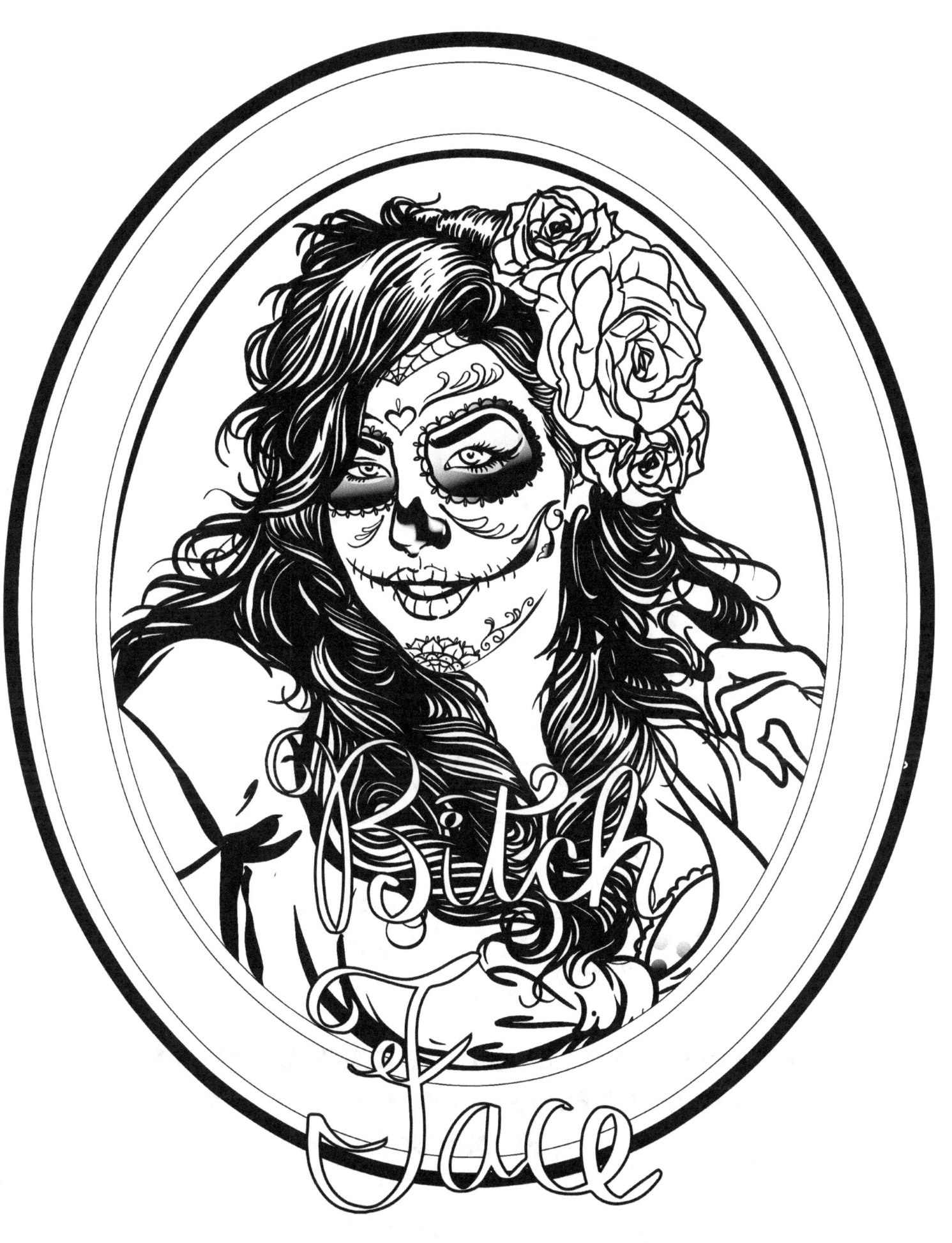

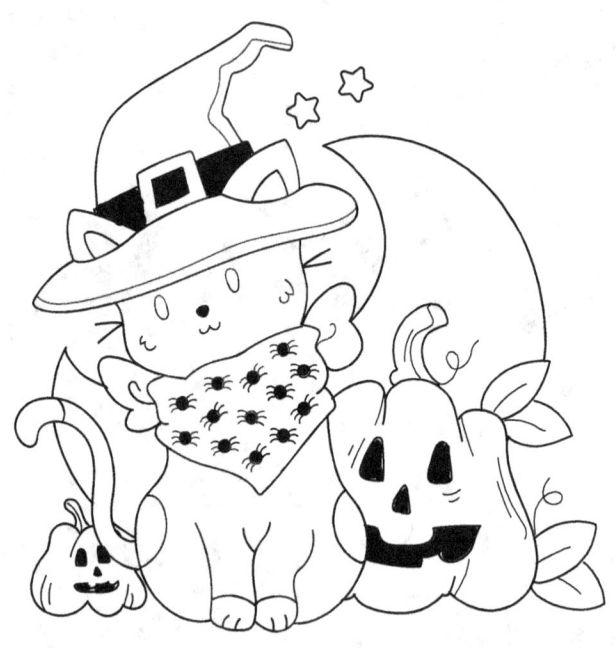

"If human Beings haD genuine Courage, they'D wear their Costumes every Day of the year, not just on Halloween."

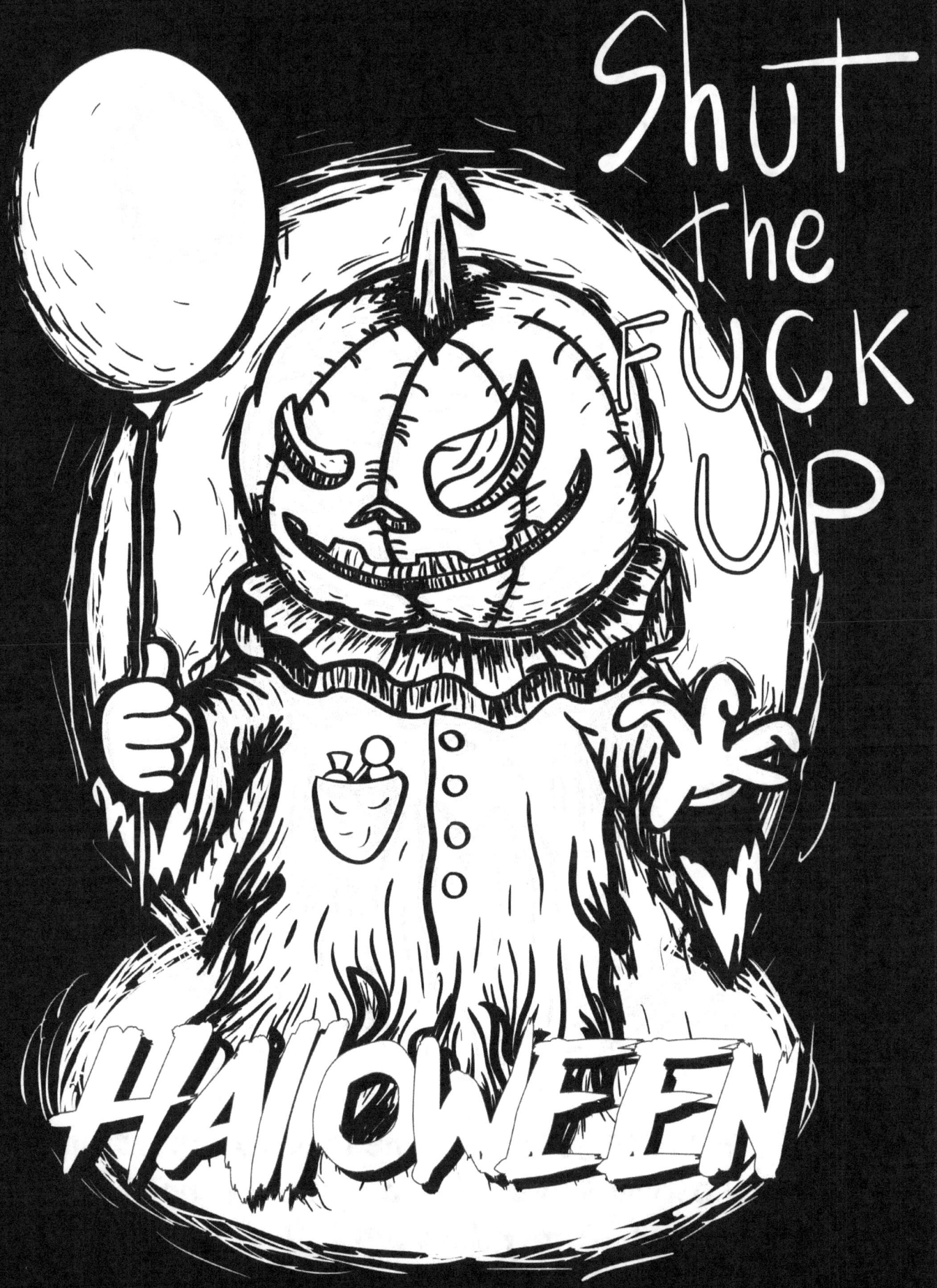

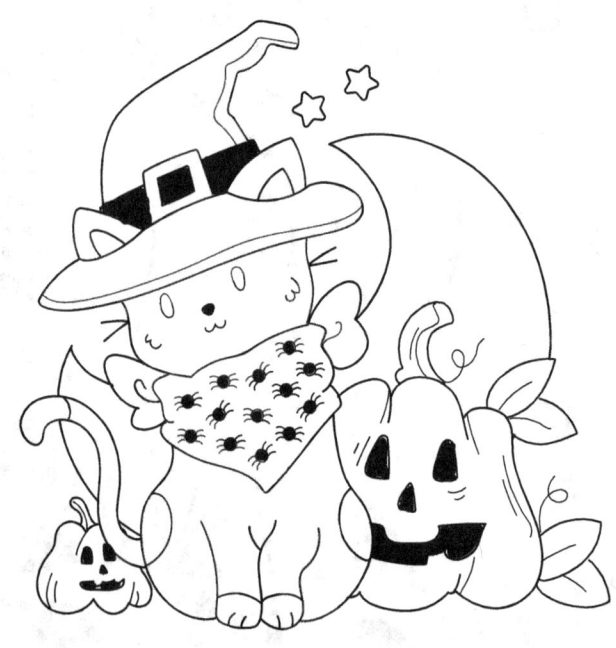

"If human Beings had genuine Courage, they'D wear their Costumes every Day of the year, not just on Halloween."

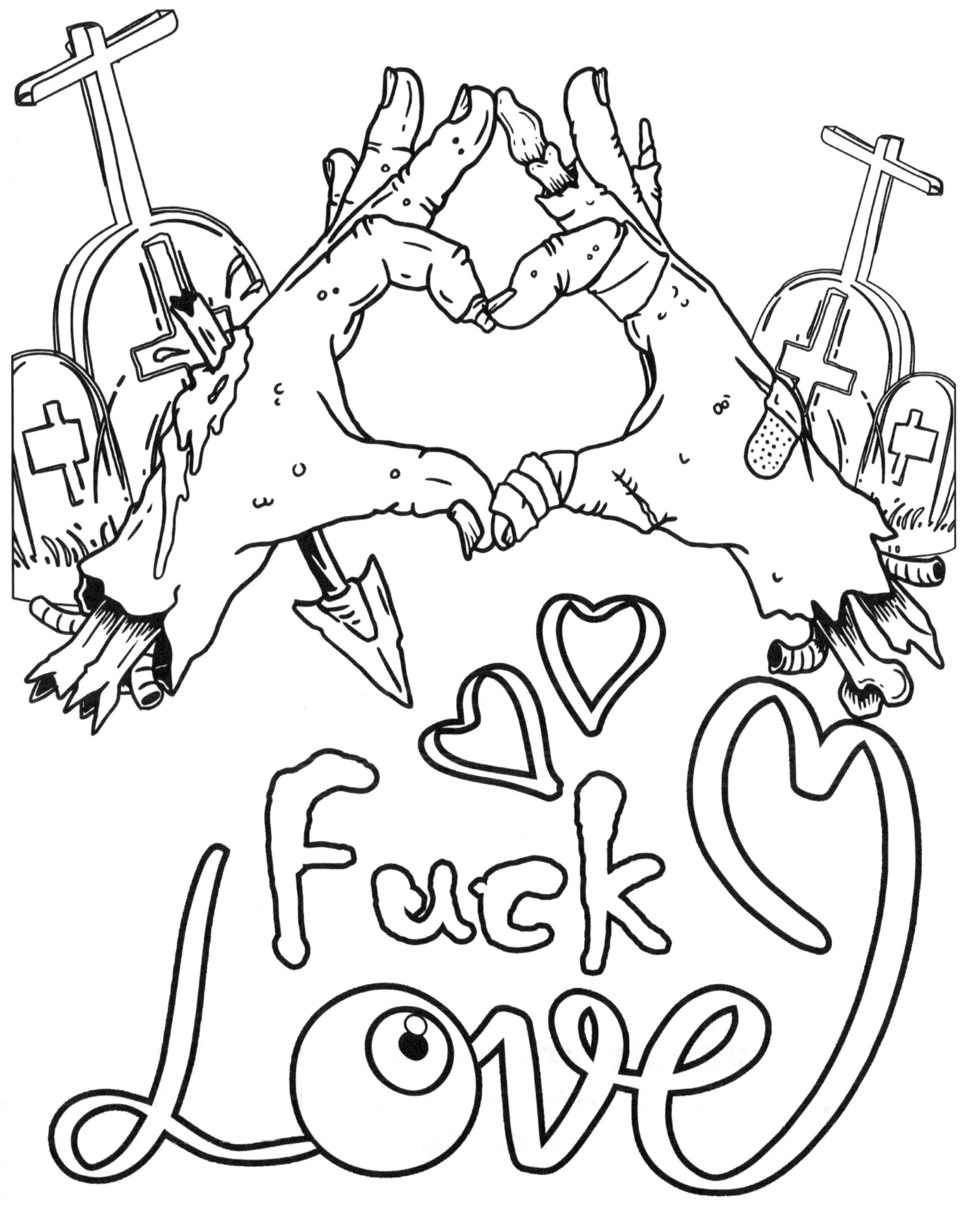

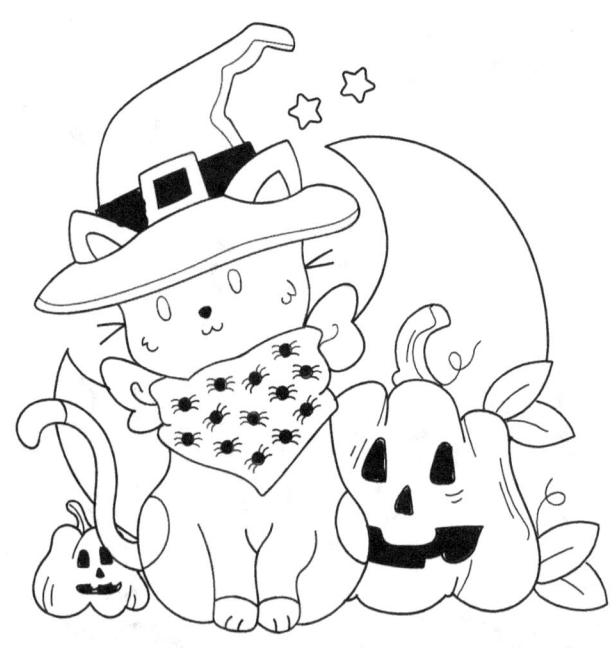

"If human Beings had genuine Courage, they'D wear their Costumes every Day of the year, not just on Halloween."

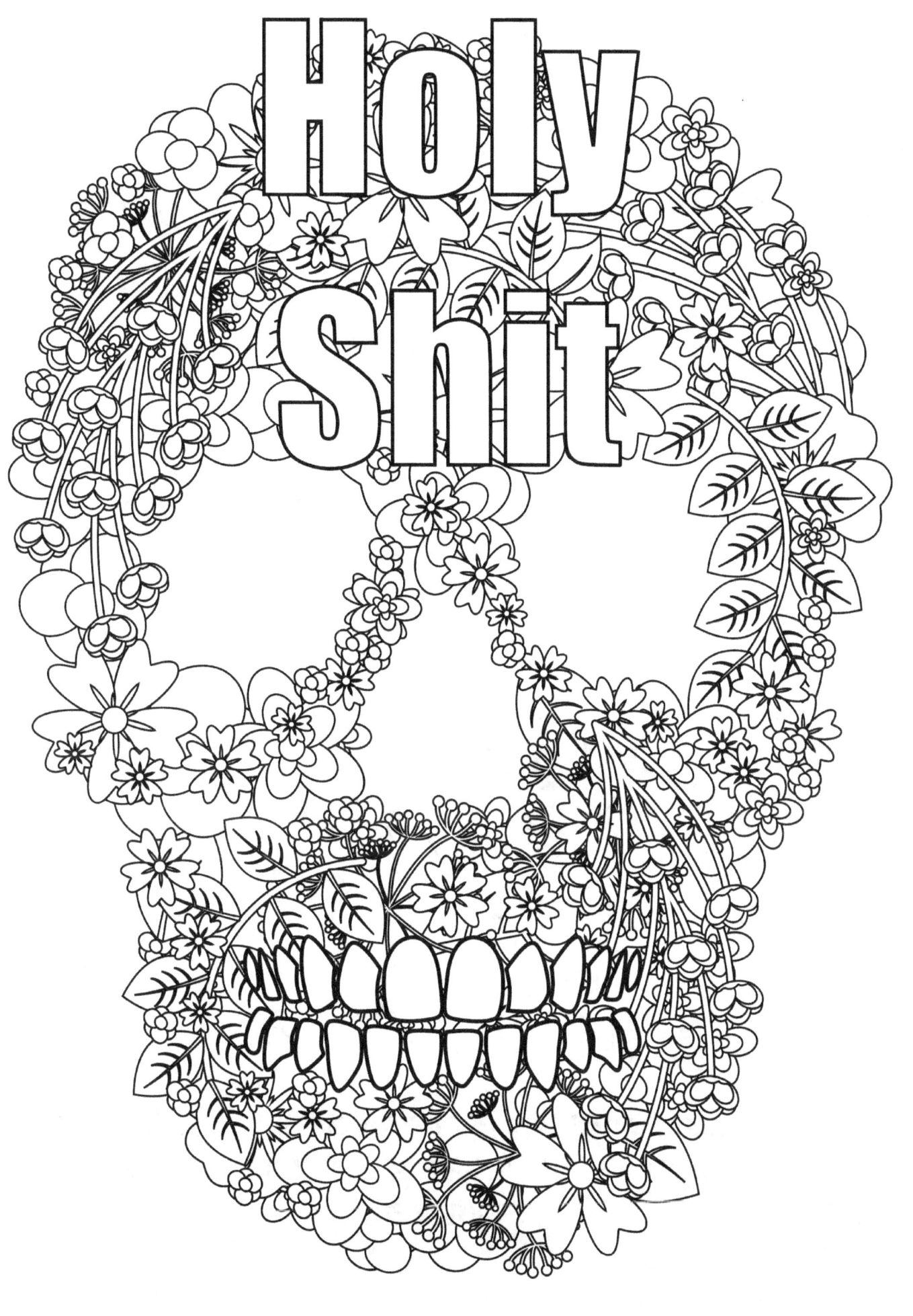

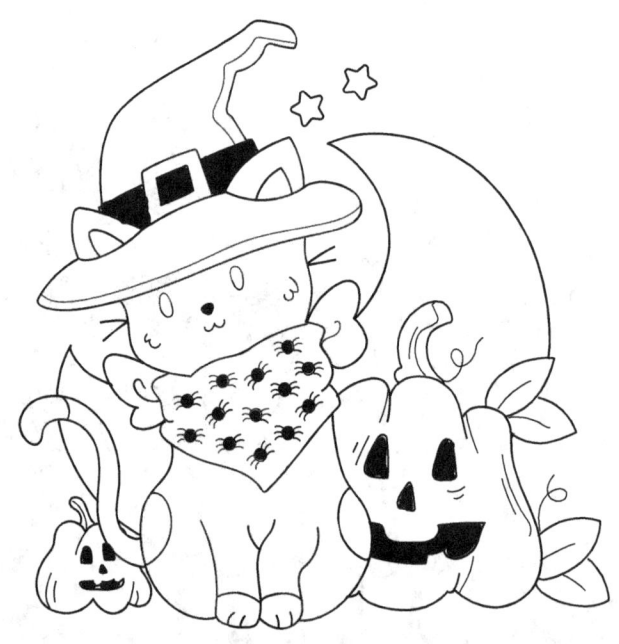

"If human Beings had genuine Courage, they'D wear
their Costumes every Day of the year, not just on
Halloween."

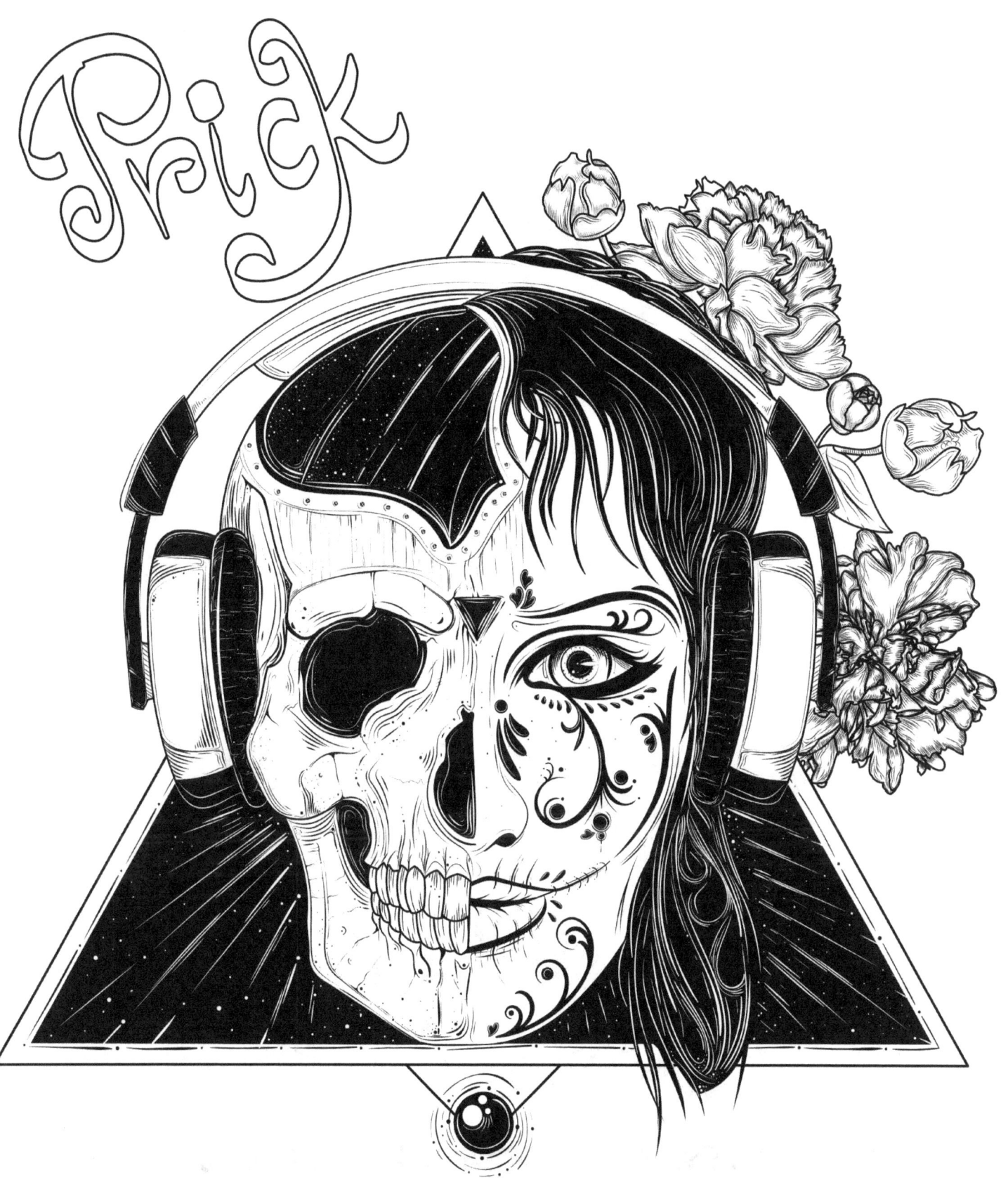

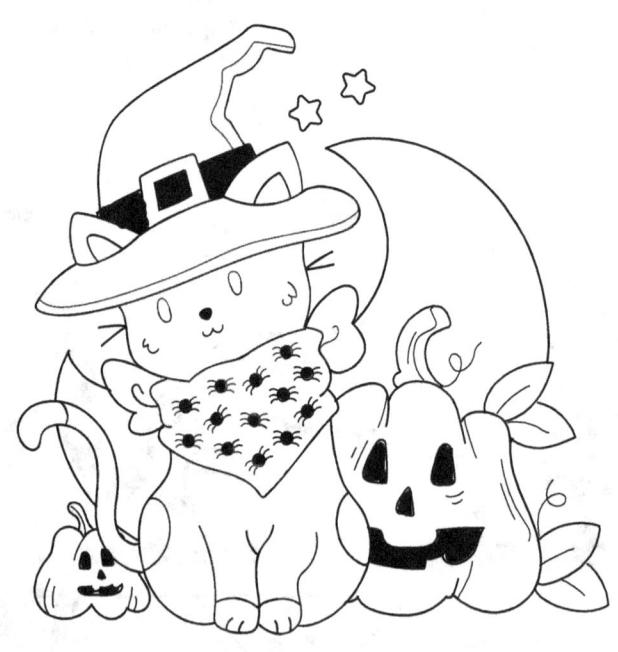

"If human Beings had genuine Courage, they'd wear their Costumes every Day of the year, not just on Halloween."

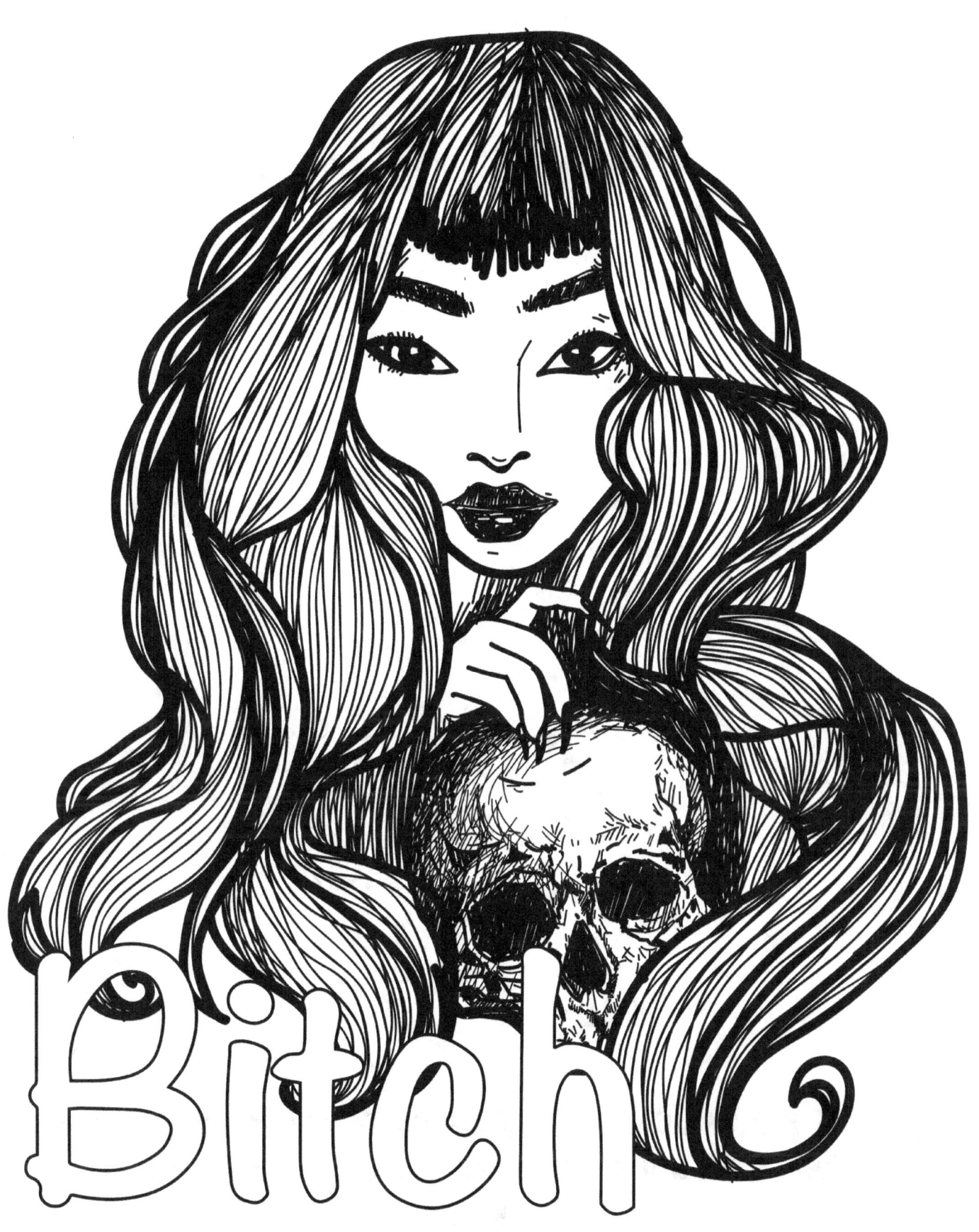

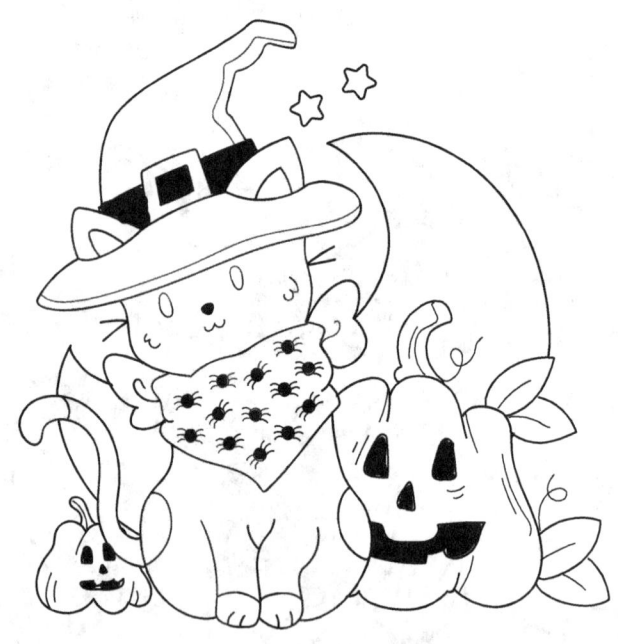

"If human Beings had genuine Courage, they'D wear their Costumes every Day of the year, not just on Halloween."

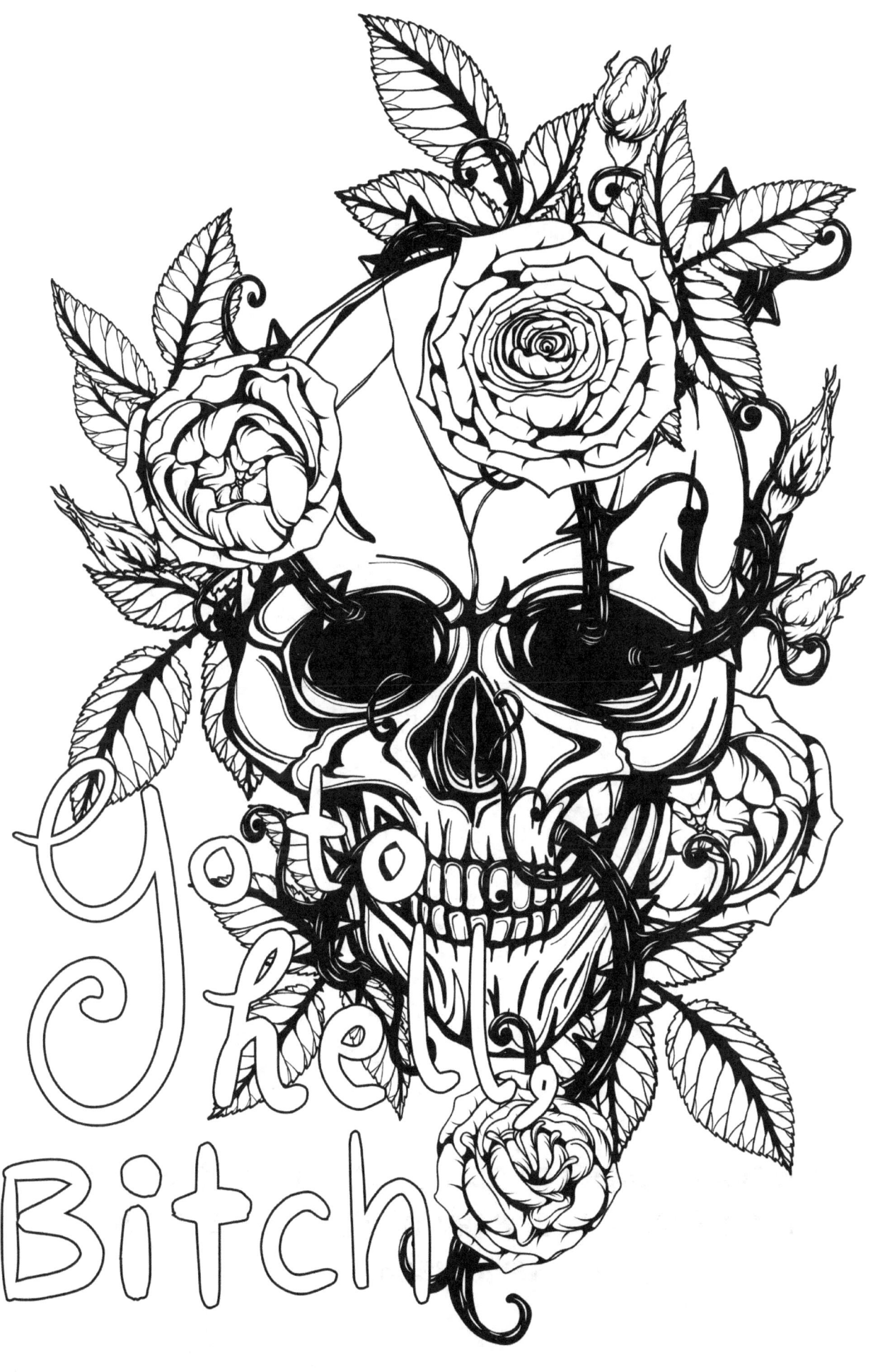

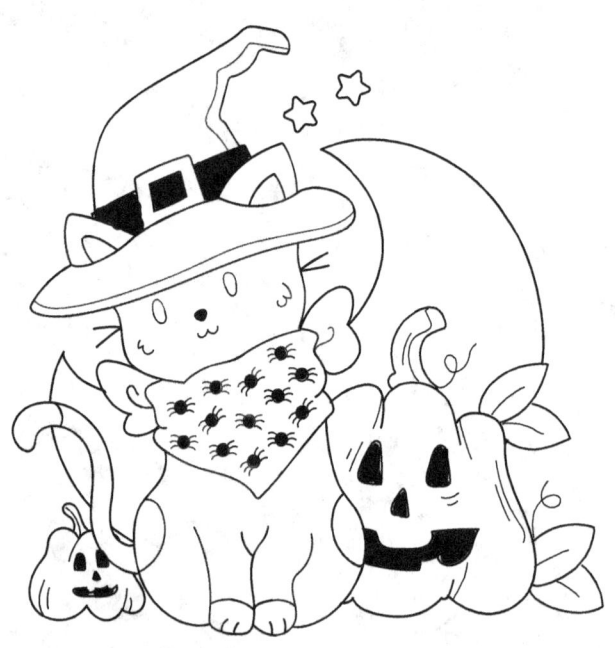

"If human Beings had genuine Courage, they'D wear their Costumes every Day of the year, not just on Halloween."

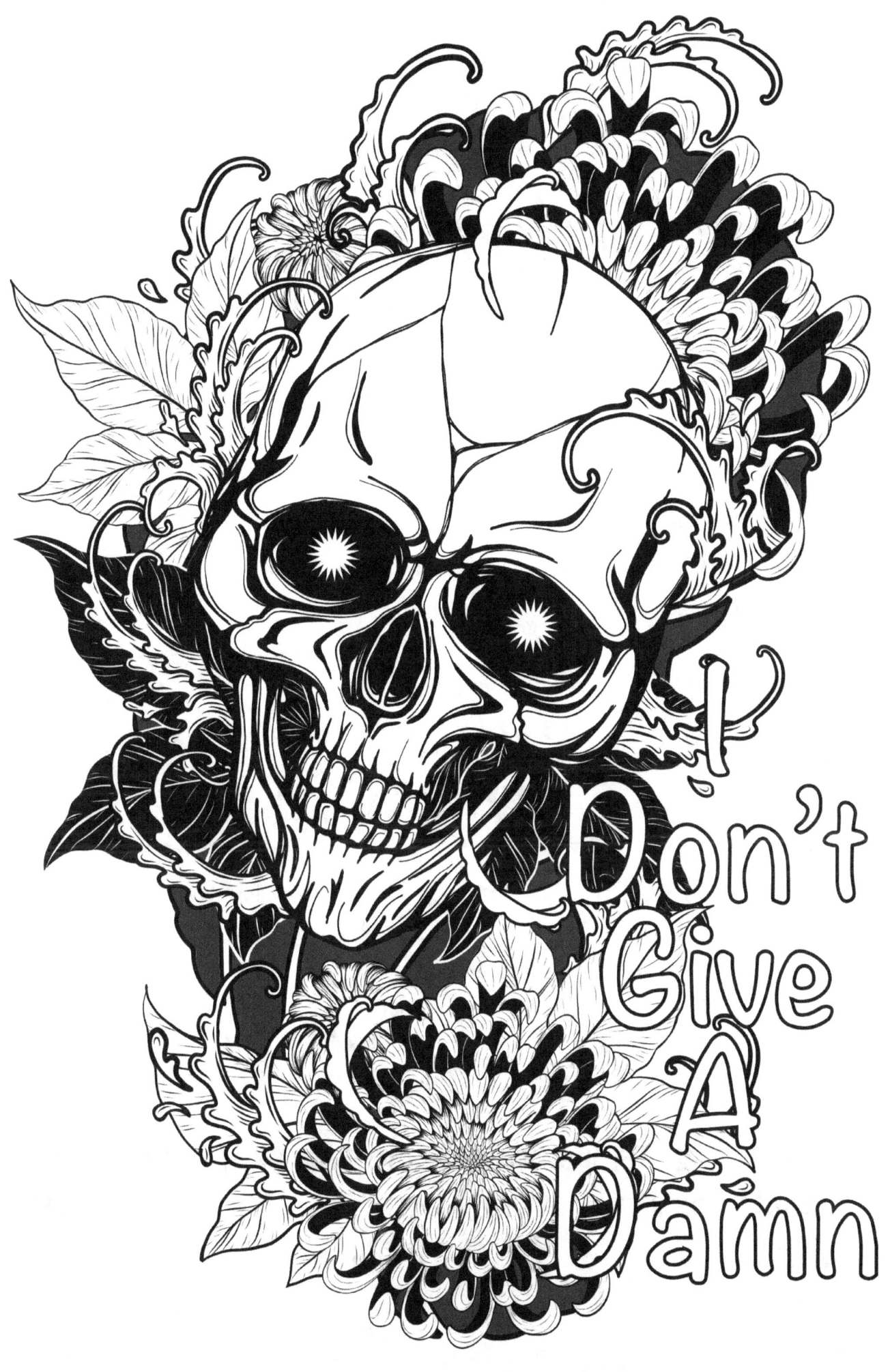

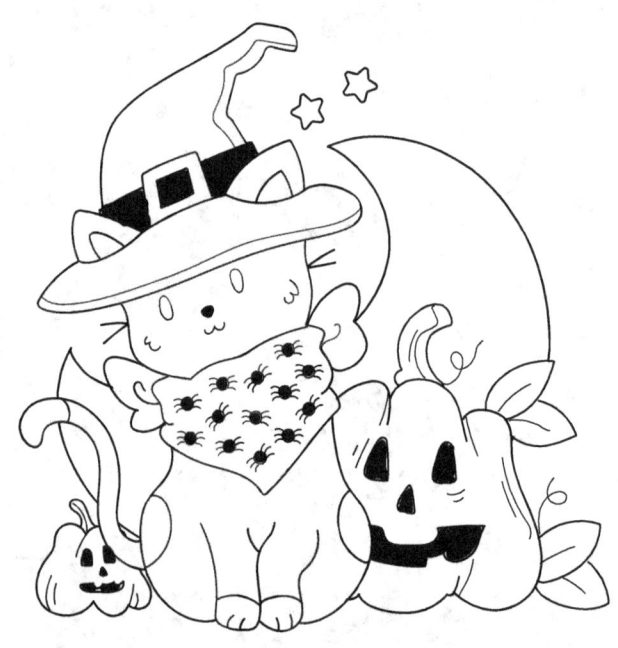

"If human Beings haD genuine Courage, they'D wear their Costumes every Day of the year, not just on Halloween."

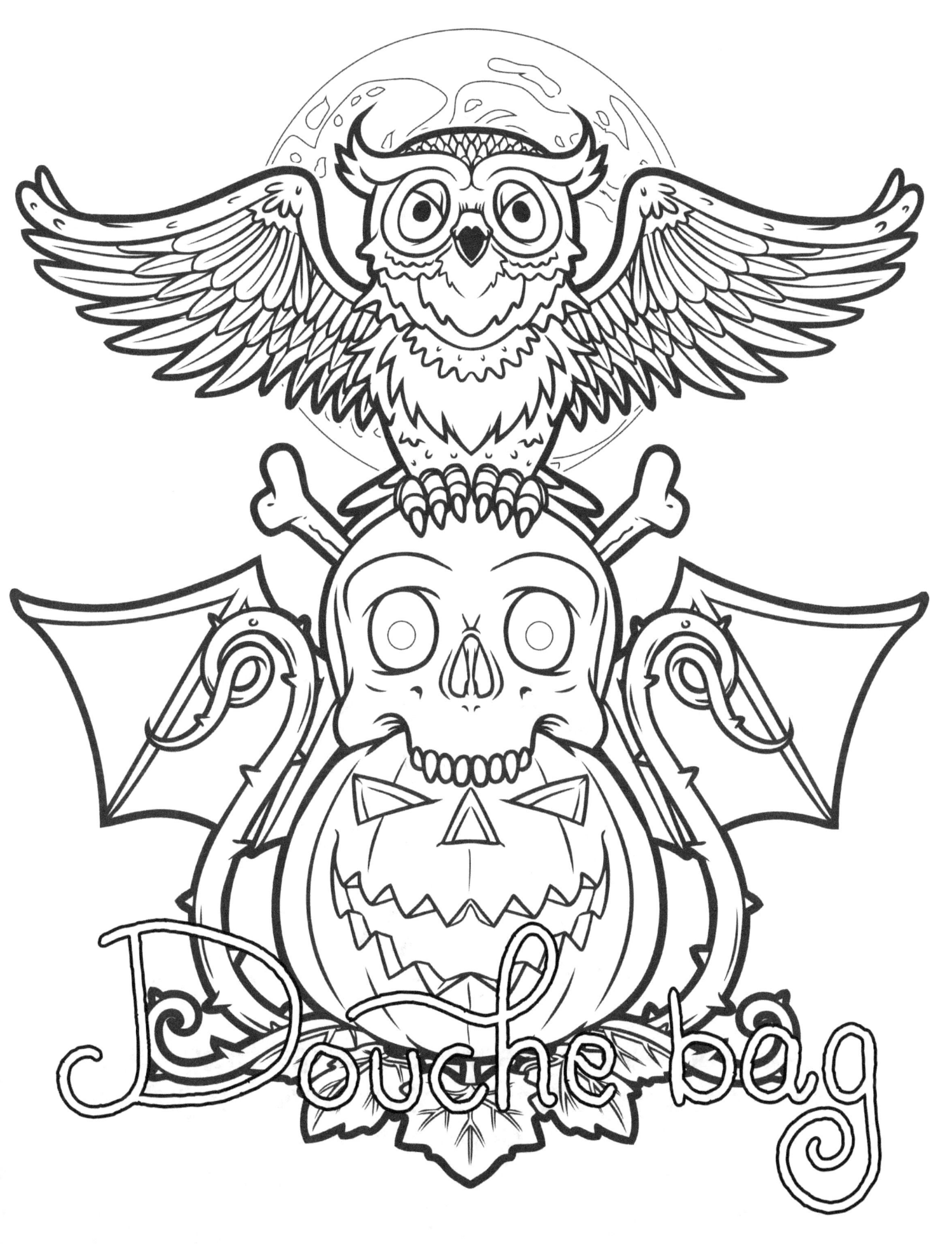

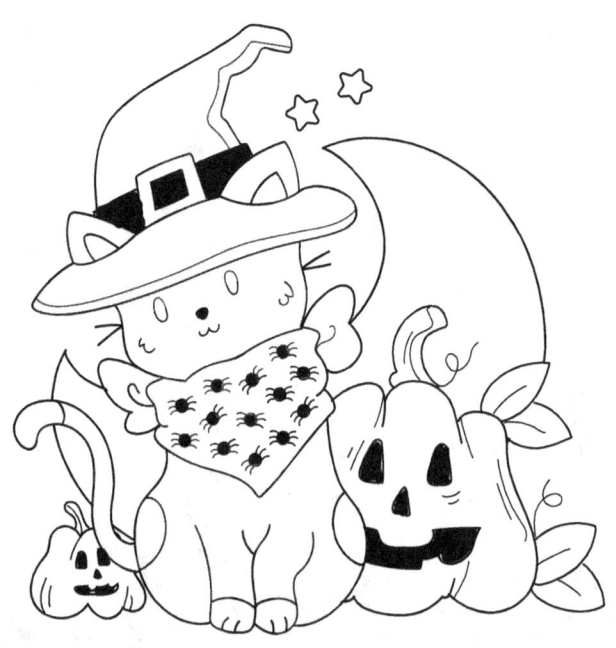

"If human Beings had genuine Courage, they'd wear their Costumes every Day of the year, not just on Halloween."

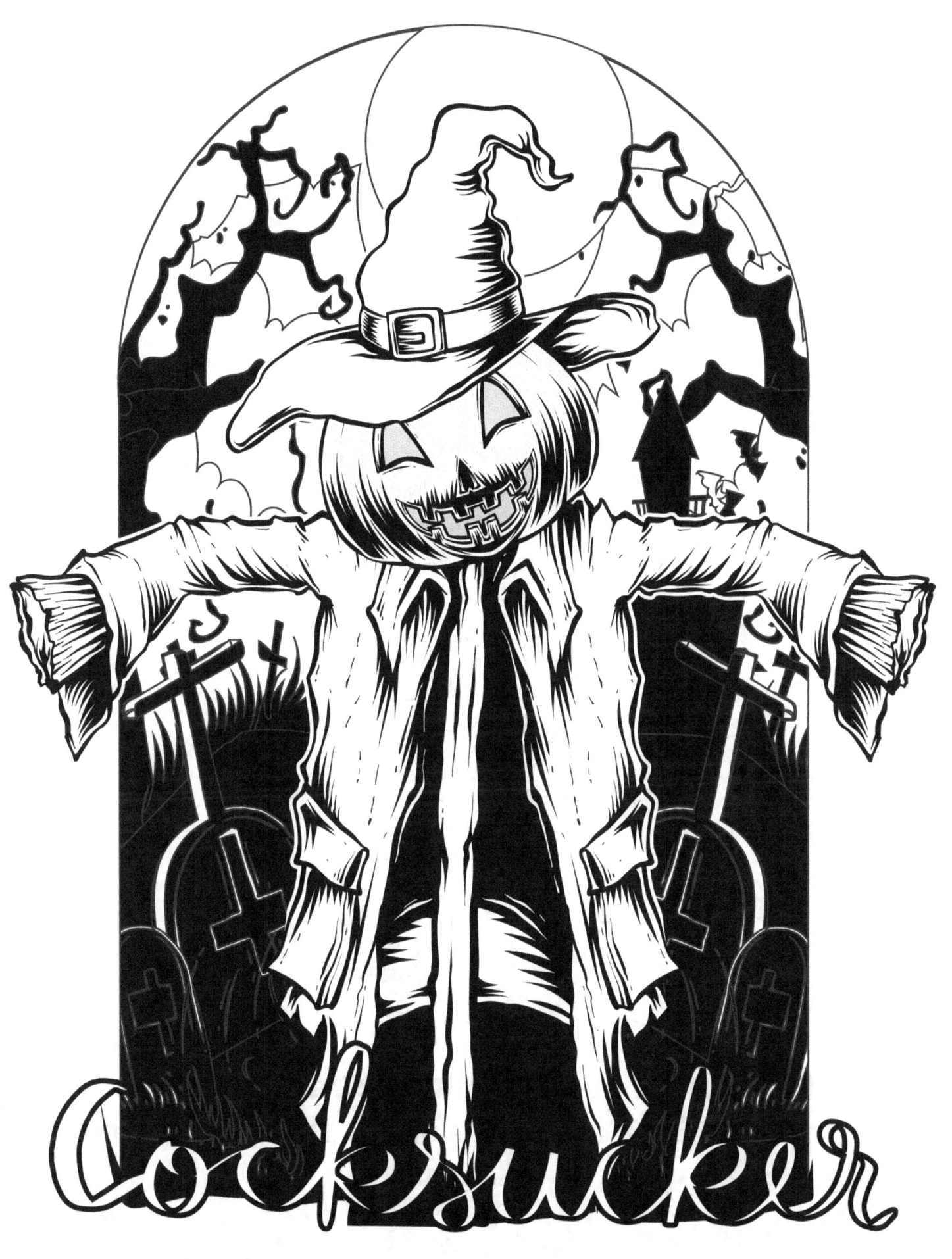

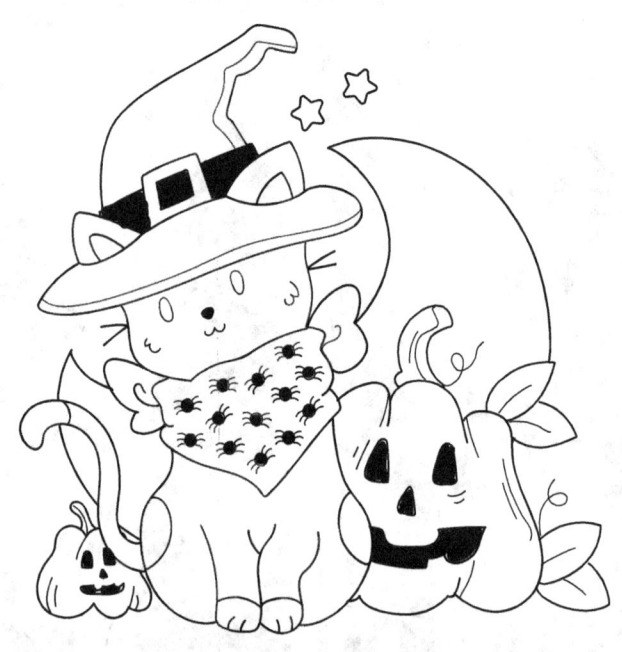

"If human Beings had genuine Courage, they'd wear their Costumes every Day of the year, not just on Halloween."

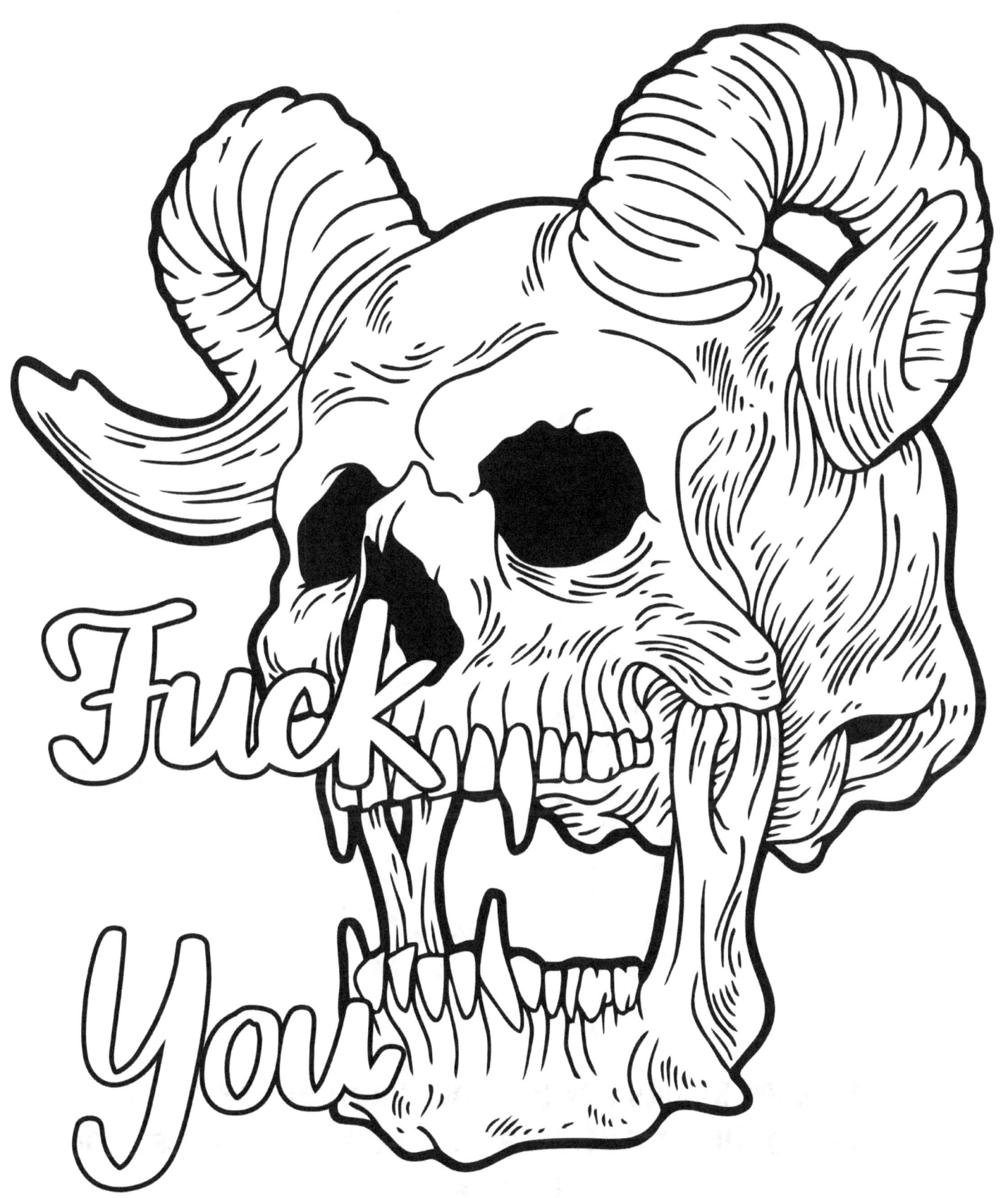

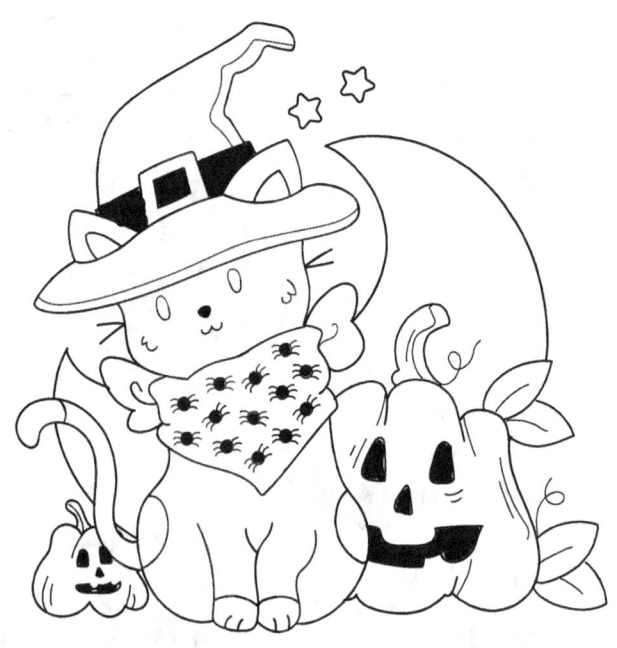

"If human Beings had genuine Courage, they'd wear their Costumes every Day of the year, not just on Halloween."

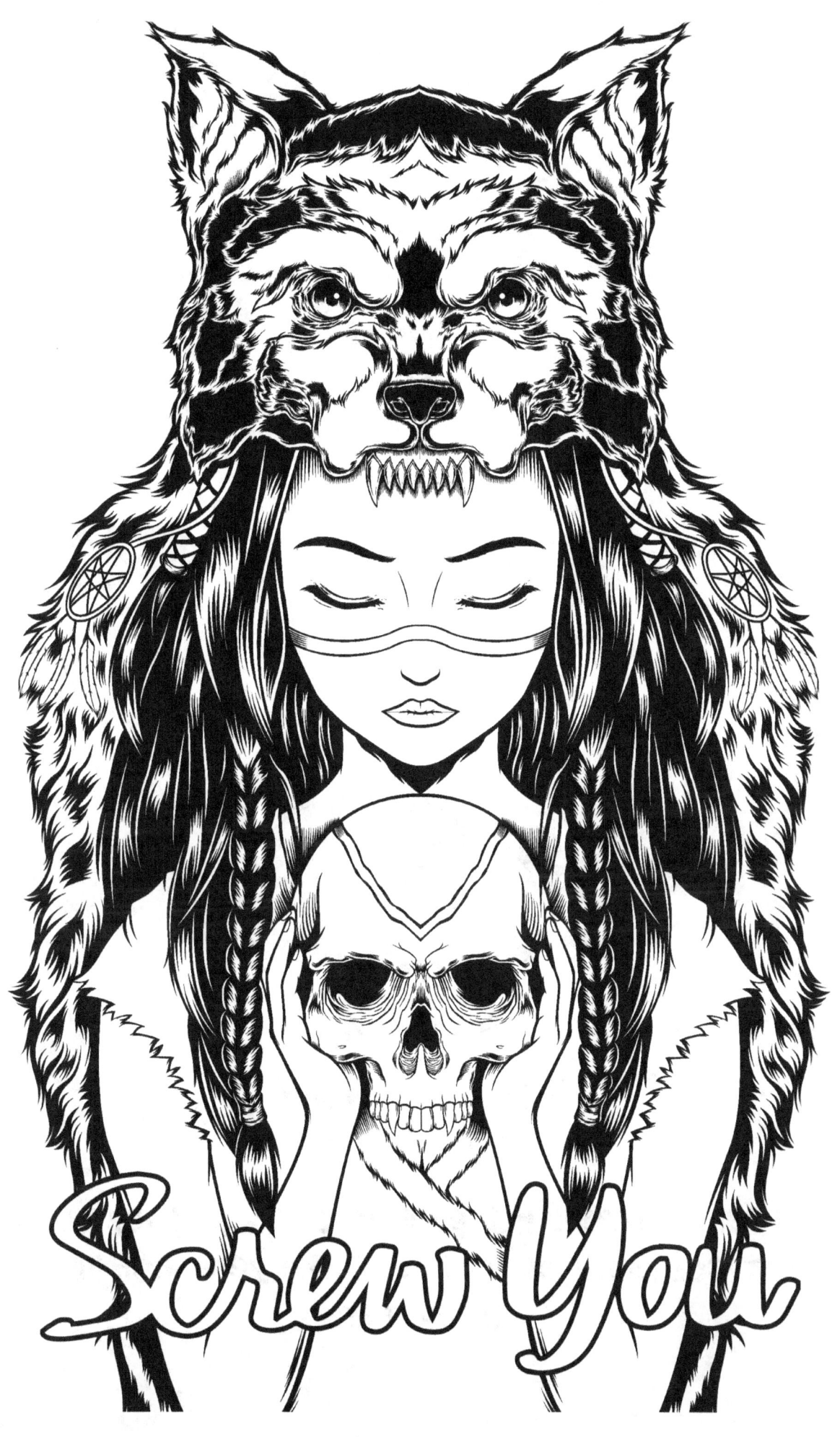

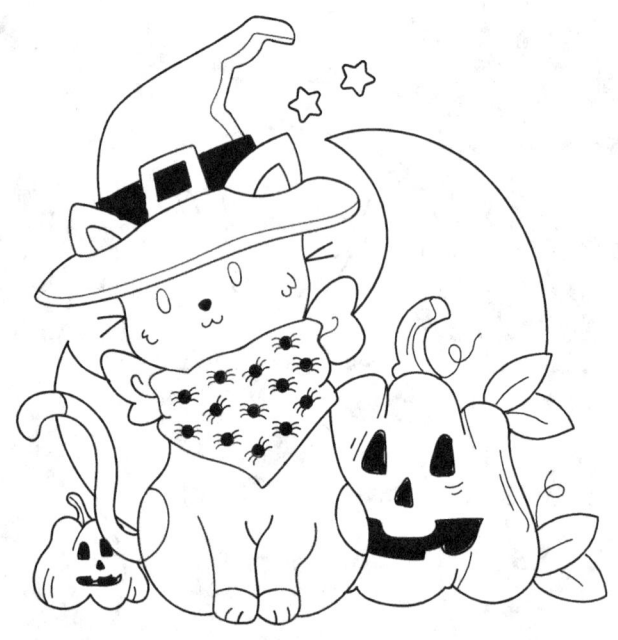

"If human Beings had genuine Courage, they'D wear their Costumes every Day of the year, not just on Halloween."

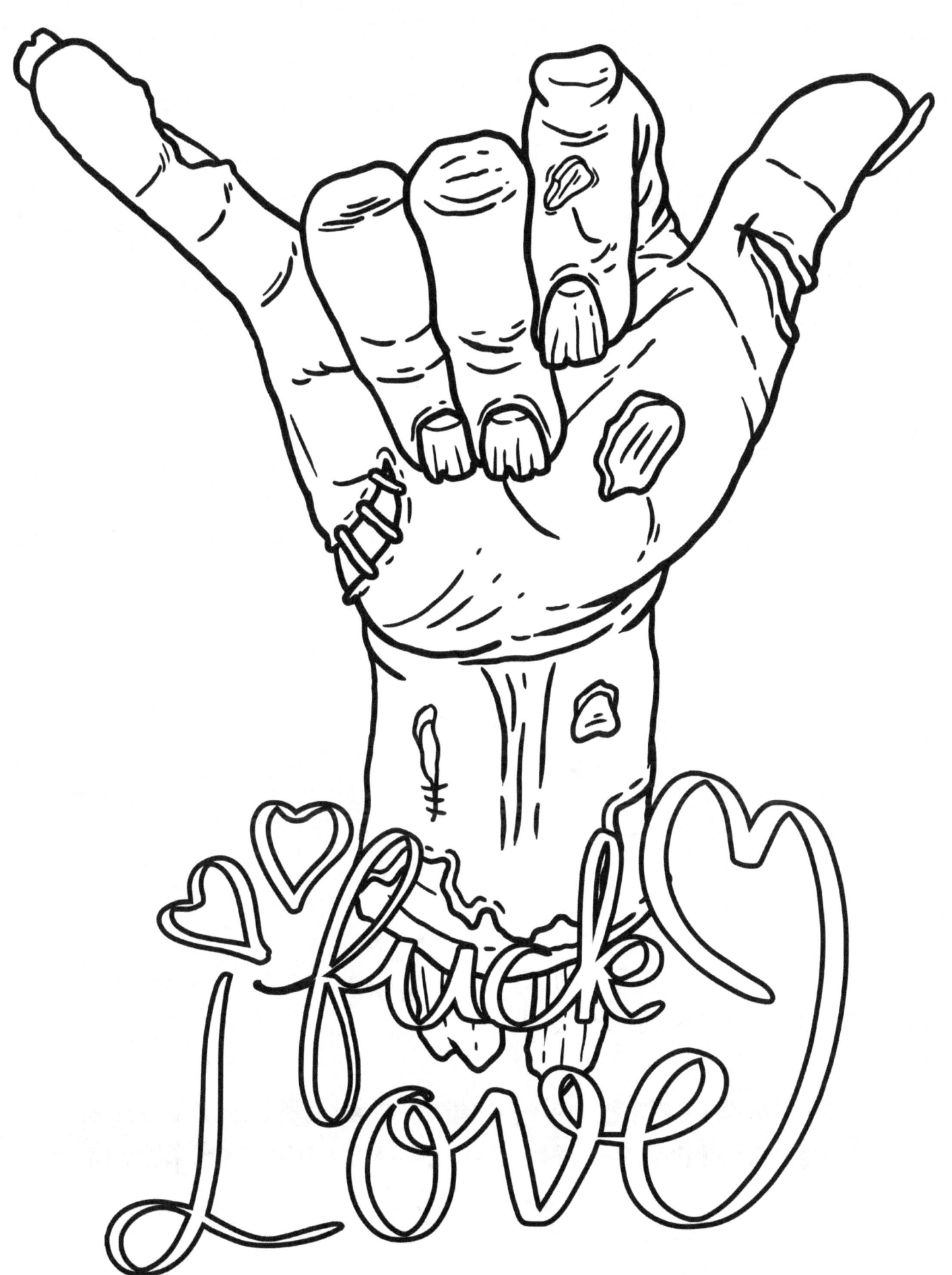

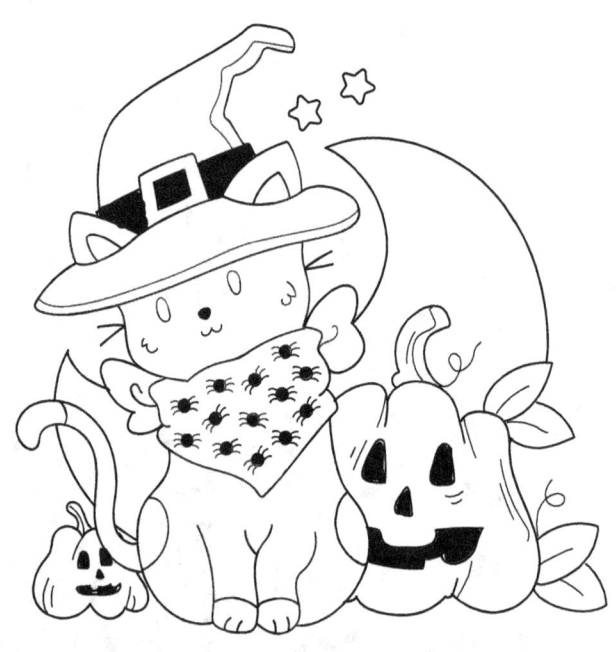

"If human Beings haD genuine Courage, they'D wear their Costumes every Day of the year, not just on Halloween."

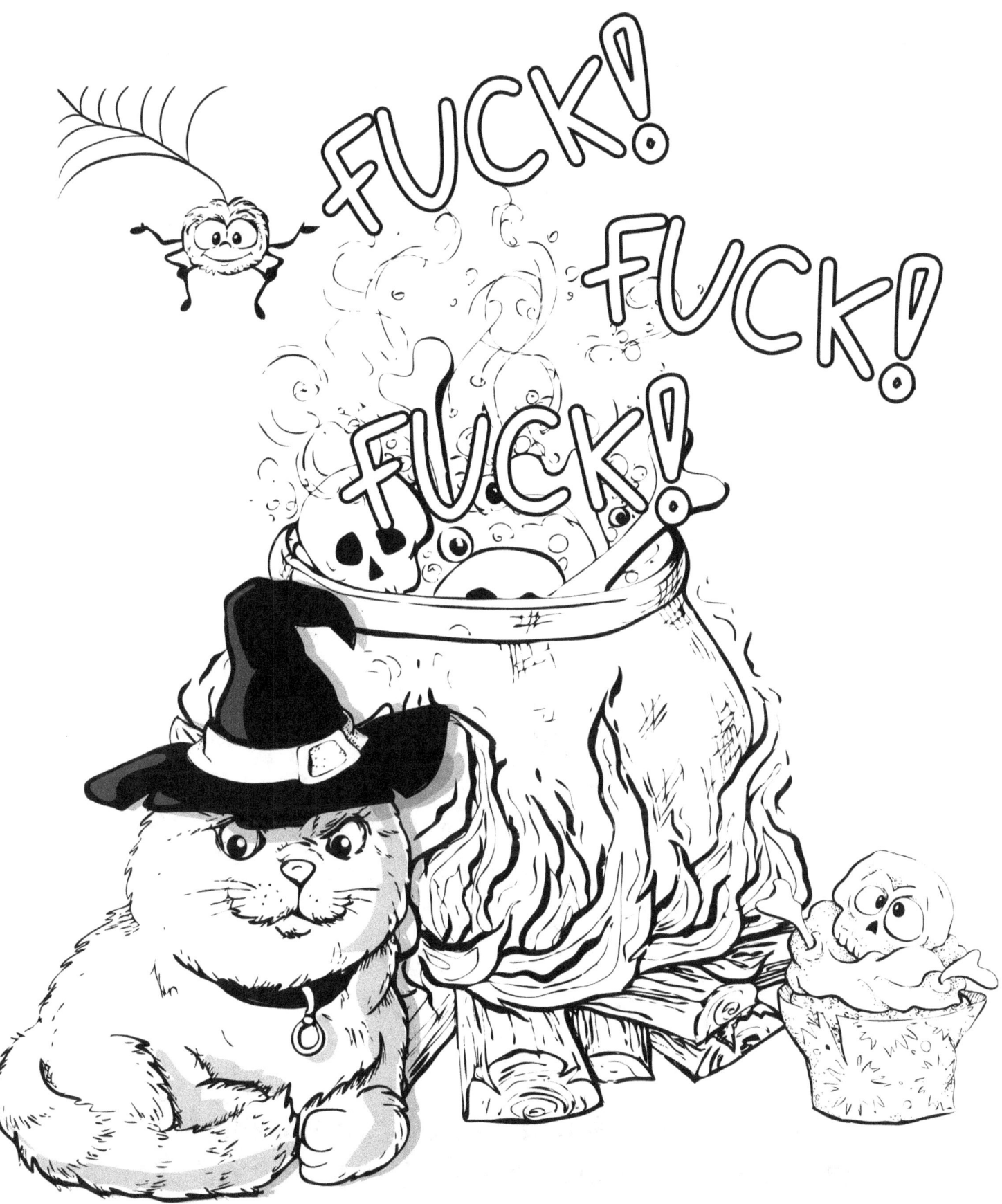

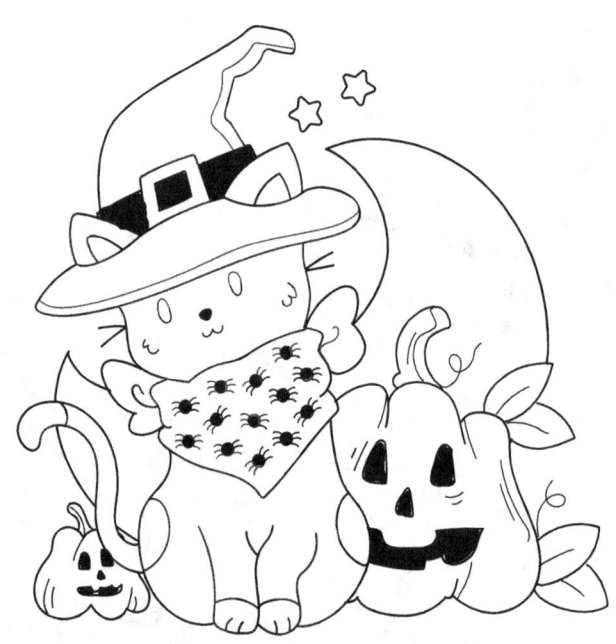

"If human Beings had genuine Courage, they'D wear their Costumes every Day of the year, not just on Halloween."

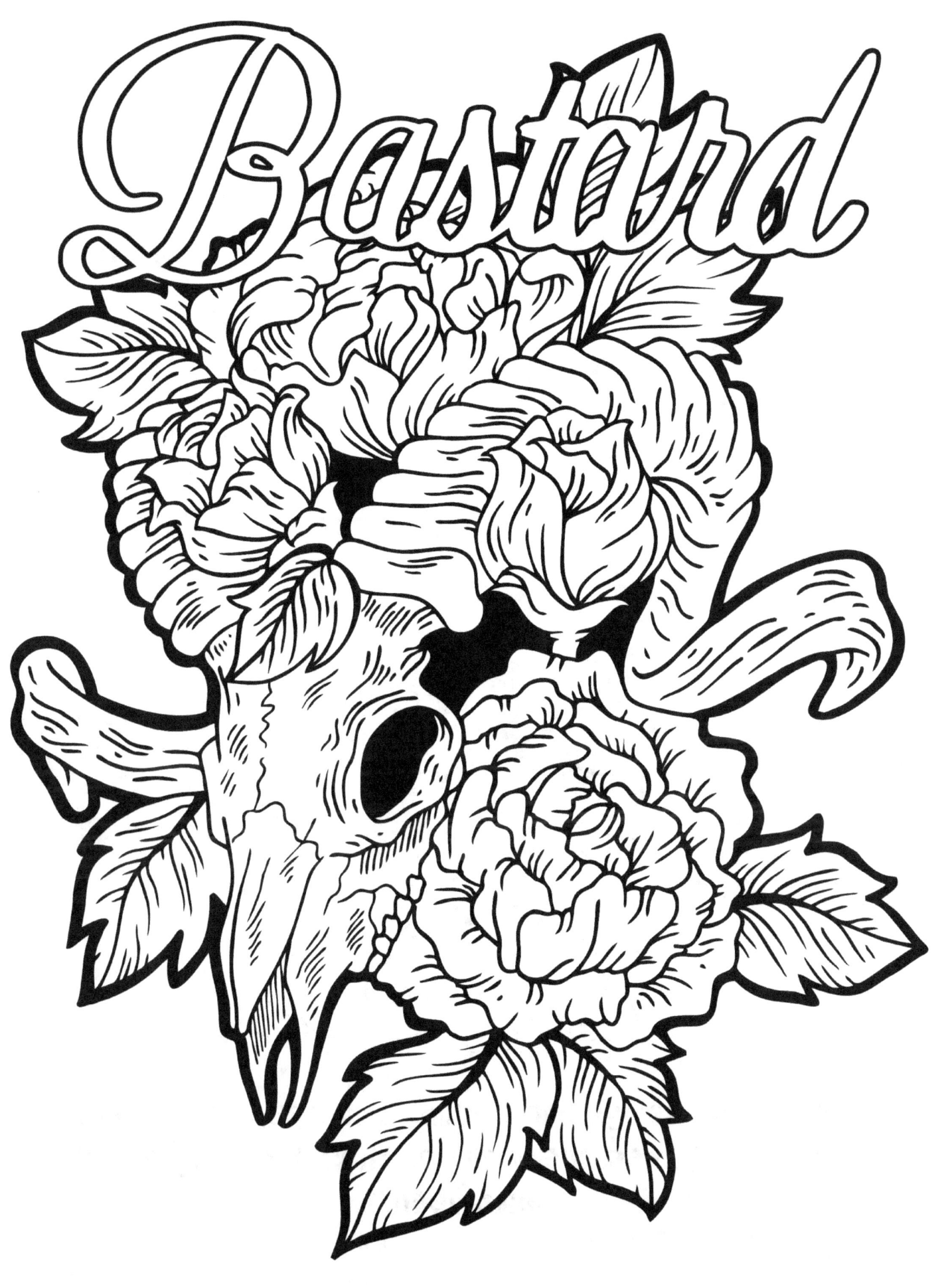

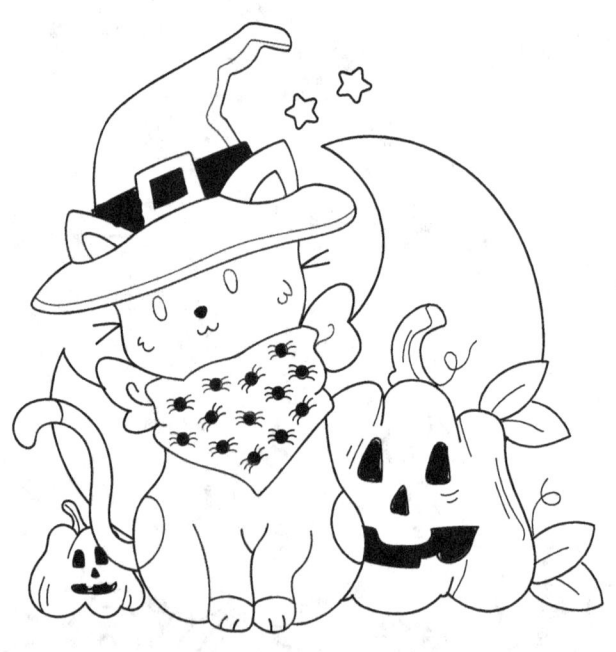

"If human Beings haD genuine Courage, they'D wear their Costumes every Day of the year, not just on Halloween."

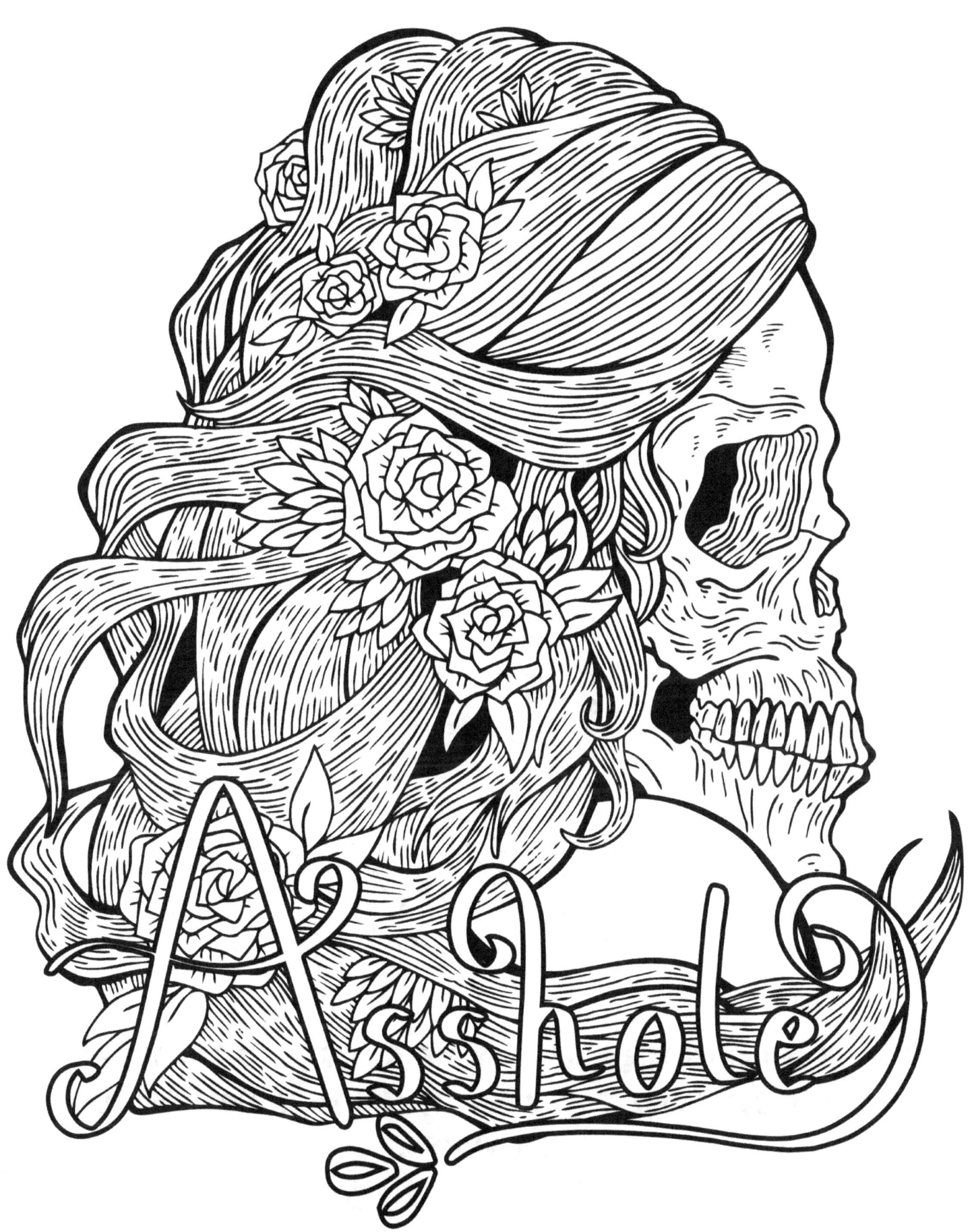

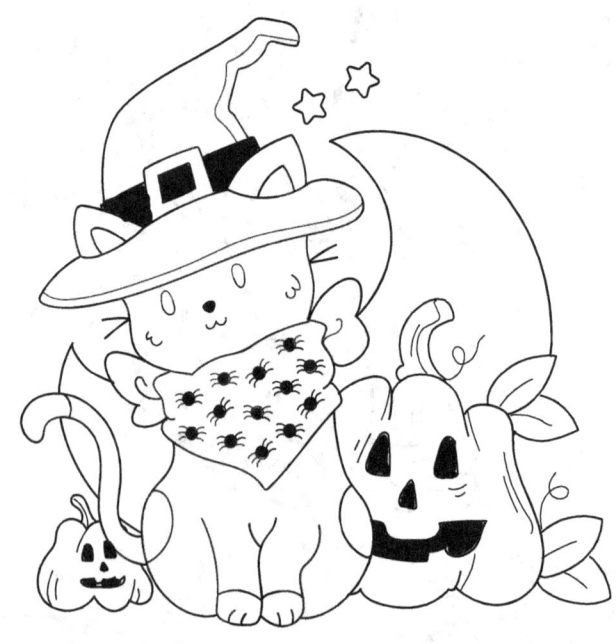

"If human Beings had genuine Courage, they'D wear their Costumes every Day of the year, not just on Halloween."

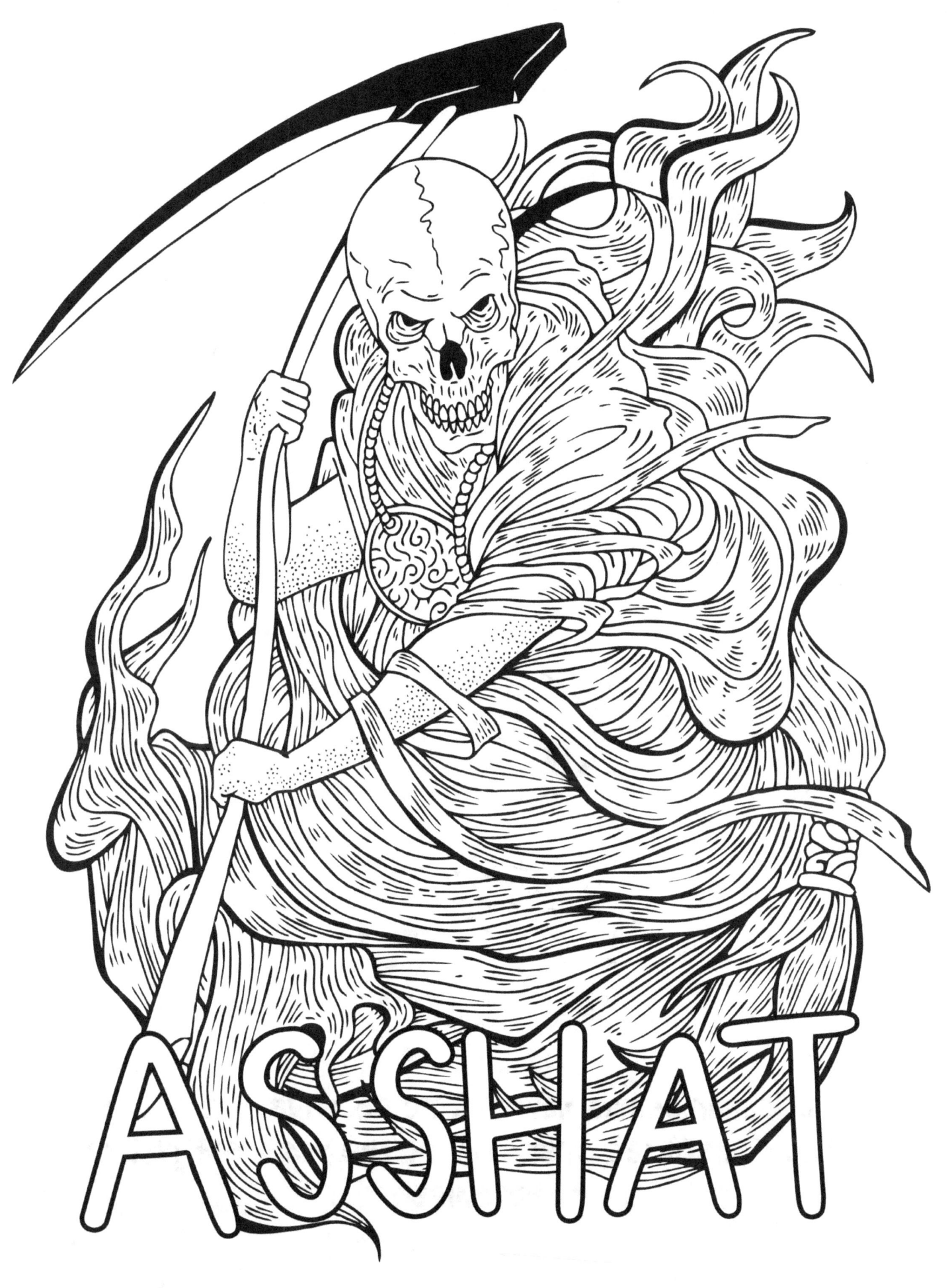

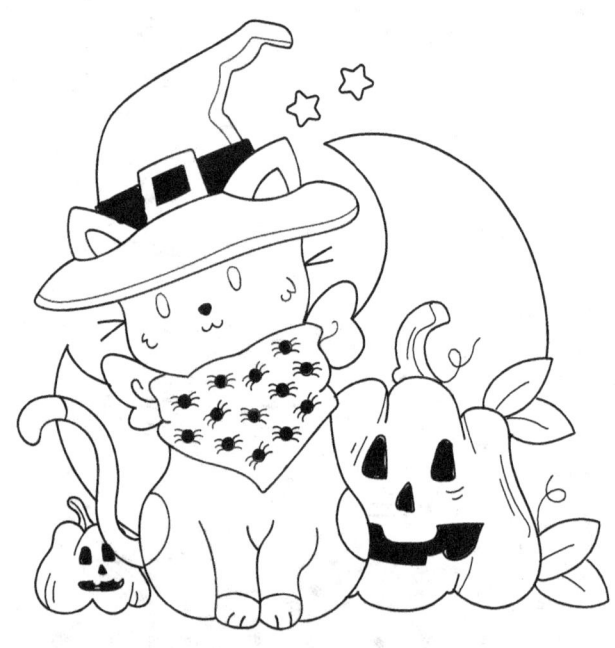

"If human Beings haD genuine Courage, they'D wear their Costumes every Day of the year, not just on Halloween."

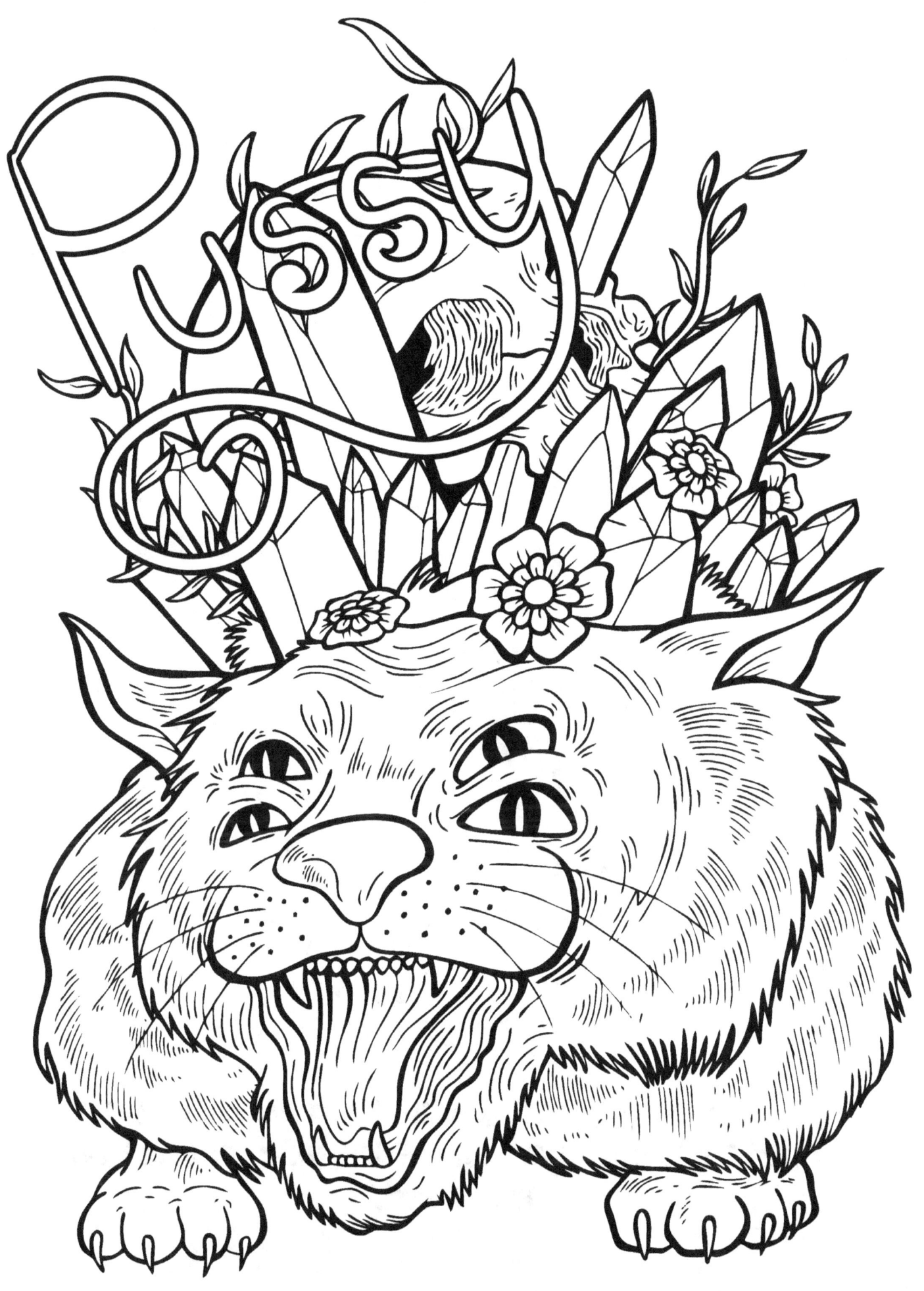

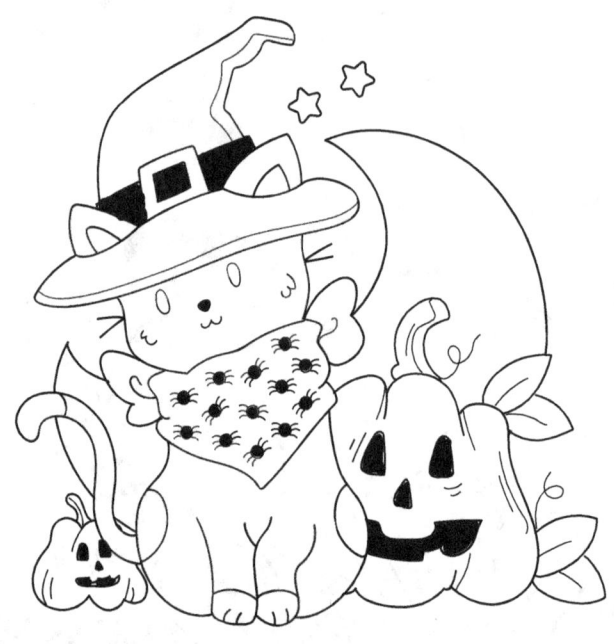

"If human Beings had genuine Courage, they'D wear their Costumes every Day of the year, not just on Halloween."

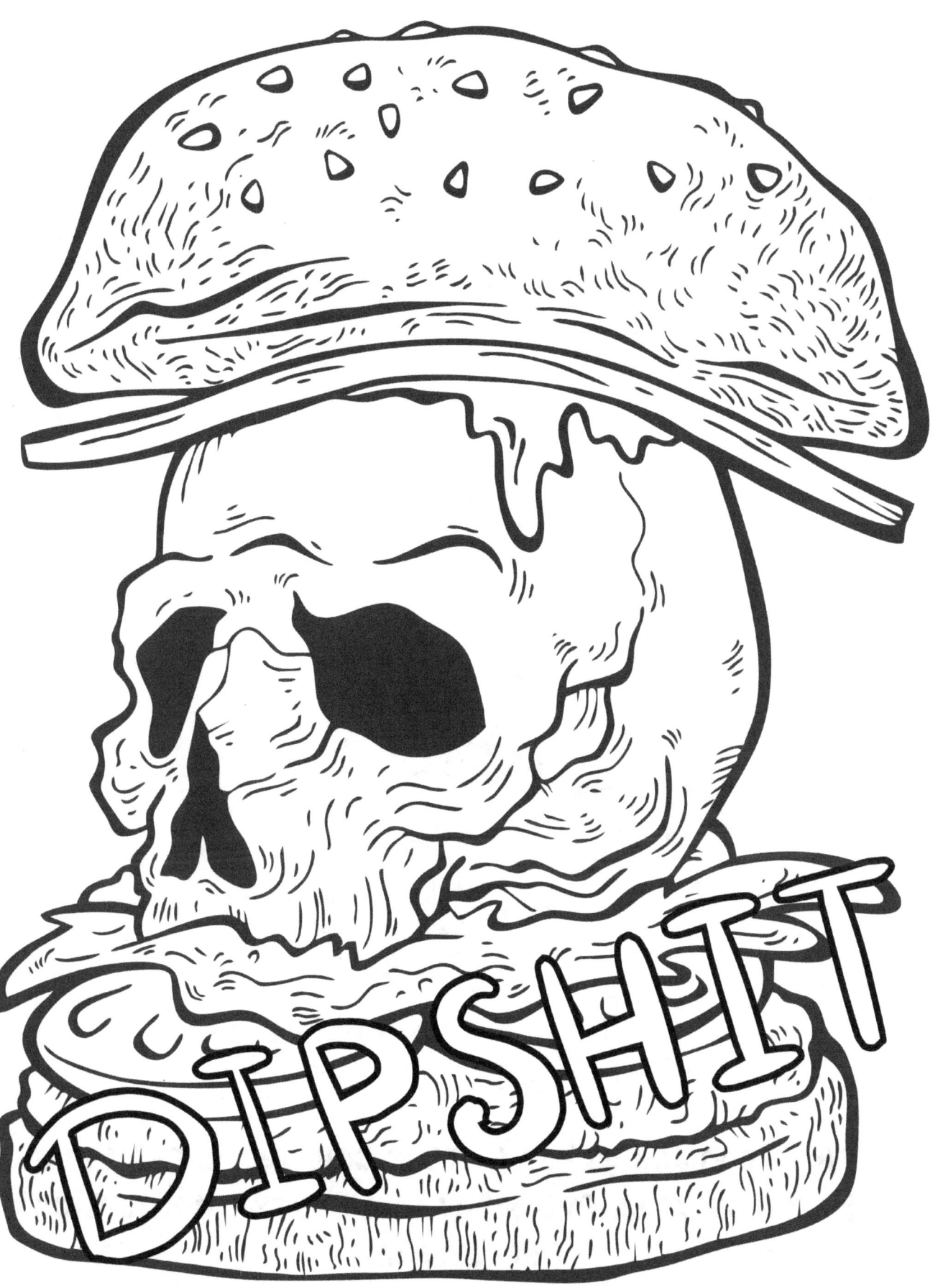

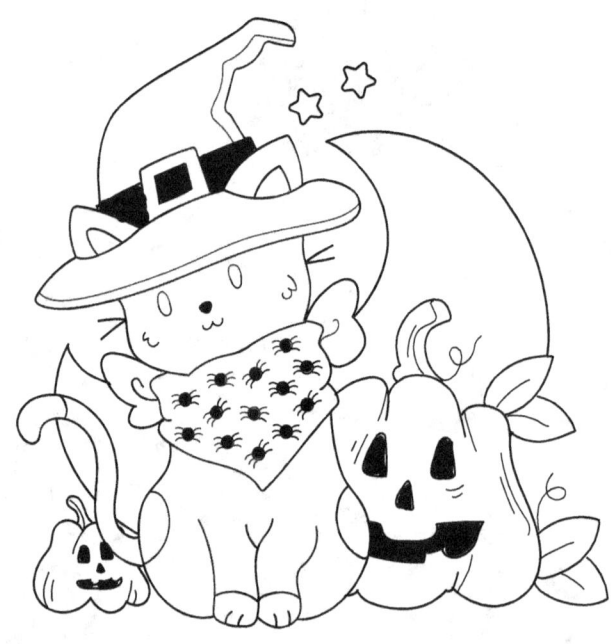

"If human Beings had genuine Courage, they'D wear their Costumes every Day of the year, not just on Halloween."

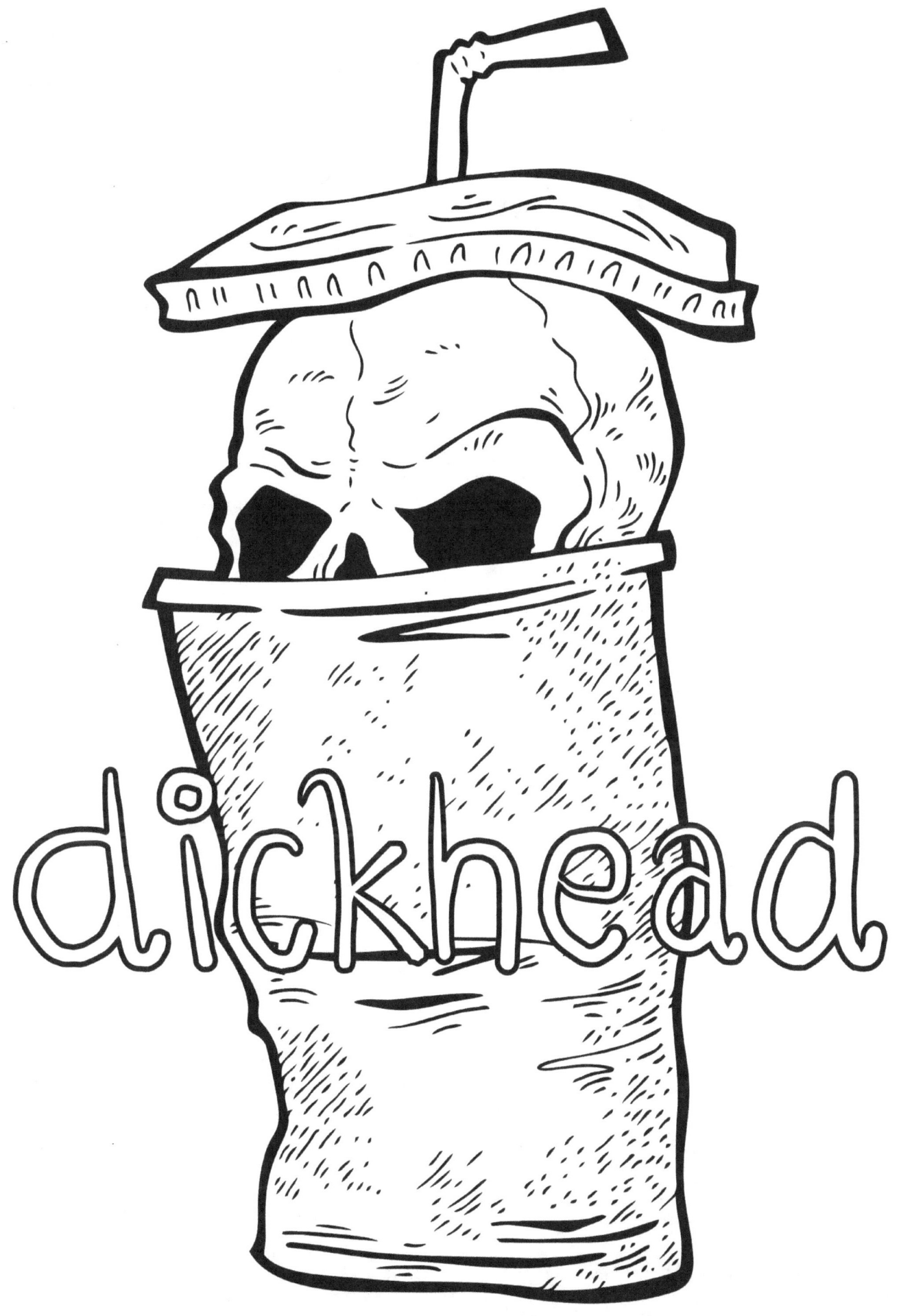